ROBERT CRAWFORD

Can We Ever Kill?

DARTON·LONGMAN+TODD

First published in Great Britain in 1991
by HarperCollinsReligious

This edition published in 2000 by
Darton, Longman and Todd Ltd
I Spencer Court
140–142 Wandsworth High Street
London SW18 4JJ

ISBN 0-232-52358-4

A catalogue record for this book is available
from the British Library.

Designed by Sandie Boccacci
Phototypeset in 10.75/14pt Sabon by Intype London Ltd
Printed and bound in Great Britain by
Redwood Books, Trowbridge, Wiltshire

To Pat and Paul with love

Contents

Introduction

The purpose of this book is to consider issues which cause heartache, disillusionment and despair. Suicide, euthanasia, abortion, capital punishment and war raise in acute form the killing question: Is it wrong to terminate or prevent life?

Newspapers and television feature the tragic stories. A mother tries to understand why her son, who had just gained his degree, committed suicide. Husbands and wives plead with their spouses to assist them to commit suicide. A murderer dies in the electric chair in the USA. Scenes of carnage resulting from bombing raise questions about wars which cause the death of civilians. Today it is the television, beaming nightly such tragedies into our living rooms which challenges us to decide about the rightness or wrongness of abortion or suicide or war or capital punishment or euthanasia. But how can we do this without some know-ledge of what religion and philosophy have said over the years? What are the arguments for and against having an abortion? Is suicide to be condemned? Why should a doctor not have the right to end the life of a patient who is being kept alive by advanced medical technology? Is there any point in prolonging a life which has lost its value? Why not bring back capital punishment for awful crimes? Is war always wrong? What about a just war?

These and other questions are discussed in this book in the light of what philosophers and religions have taught but in a simple and direct way, so that the student and general reader who has little knowledge of these disciplines may understand moral arguments. As far as possible, technicalities have been avoided.

The situations described and the killing question involved form a part of suffering in general and raise the problem of how we are to view life as a whole. Is life meaningless? How should it be lived? Is life good or bad? Does death end it all? How could a good God create a world like this?

These larger questions are discussed in the last two chapters, but we start with suicide in Chapter One. It considers the claim that we have the right to dispose of our lives if we have reached the breaking point and that others should not interfere with that freedom. We reflect on the various judgements that have been made concerning the suicidal act and ask if there is a difference between taking one's life and giving it. It is argued that motive, intention and result are important in making a moral judgement.

Chapter Two examines the various forms of euthanasia and asks if all should be permitted. Insights into this problem are gleaned from philosophy, religion and medicine, and these are used to help us make some judgements. A distinction is drawn between killing someone and letting them die, and legal cases are considered in this connection. The conclusion endorsed is that while life should not be prolonged needlessly by medical technology, active termination should be avoided.

Chapter Three takes up the question of abortion and asks if a woman has the right to dispose of the foetus in her womb in whatever way she thinks best. It reviews the various ideas concerning the moral status of the foetus and reflects on the difficulties posed by them. A basic question is whether we are to regard the foetus as a person or as a potential person. It is seen that various philosophical and theological perspectives will affect our attitudes to this problem. To add to the difficulties, we now have *in vitro* fertilisation and research on embryos, about which certain decisions have been made by various governments throughout the world. It is argued that abortion is a very serious matter and that if it is necessary it should take place as soon as possible after conception. The whole question should be approached in a spirit of love and understanding.

Chapter Four weighs the strengths and weaknesses of the arguments for and against capital punishment and argues that deterrence does not have the strength of the traditional retributive ground. But this must exclude any thought of revenge and in the judicial process must be seen as setting right the inequality and injustice which has resulted from murder. The punishment could only apply to aggravated murder, and there remains the problem of how we might decide what particular forms of such a murder deserve the ultimate penalty. The strongest argument against the death penalty stems from the fear that an innocent man or woman might be hanged.

Chapter Five widens the issue of killing from the individual case to the corporate killing that is war. It reviews pacifism, the just war, the holy war and the awful effect of a possible nuclear war. While the end of the cold war between East and West and the resulting reduction of weapons have sent a wave of optimism around the world, there is still concern about the fact that other nations now possess such weapons and have threatened to use them.

It is argued that modern war becomes harder to vindicate because of the efforts of pacifists and the failure of the just war theory to apply. Advanced military technology has removed the traditional view of the splendour of war and replaced it with increased cruelty and viciousness. The world has become a global village, and the need is for nations to emerge from their narrow nationalisms and work together for justice and peace.

Chapter Six extends the discussion of the religious viewpoint by a limited discussion of the morality of religions other than Christianity. In a pluralist society this is necessary and it is interesting to see how various Faiths agree or disagree in their attitudes to these issues.

Chapter Seven asks the question, 'Is life meaningless?' Suffering, evil and death all raise questions about the meaning or meaninglessness of life, and many philosophers have concluded that life has no purpose. Others oppose this view, contending that there is a prescription for the good life which, if followed, would enable us to deal with the trials of life. These proposals are examined and criticised, but it is recognised that human beings are creatures with goals and purposes, and this raises the question of whether there could be a cosmic purpose.

Chapter Eight considers the major problems that philosophers have put forward to dispute that such an overall purpose exists. This involves a limited examination of evolutionary theory, the problem of evil and the doubts about the immortality of the soul. The arguments of Christianity in dialogue with philosophy and science are reviewed, and it is contended that no decisive case against such an overall purpose has been put forward. Such a hope reduces pessimism and enables us to endure the trials of life with a faith that is not blind but has considered the objections which can be brought against it. Much is to be gained by a dialogue between philosophy and religion on these major issues.

In this second edition of the book new examples and illustrations have been introduced and a new chapter six has been added. The chapter on war has been expanded in the light of our thinking at the end of the twentieth century. I wish to acknowledge my debt to the course team of the Open University course 'Life and Death' (A310) and to the helpful books which they have written on each of the moral problems. Readers of this book are referred to them for a more detailed discussion of the philosophical approach. While reaching a different conclusion, I am indebted to Oswald Hanfling's writing on the meaning of life. Team members Diane Collinson and Rosalind Hursthouse read chapters of the first edition of the book and made helpful comments. I am grateful for these and would also like to thank Stuart Brown of the Open University, David Lamb of the University of Manchester and Duncan Forrester of the University of Edinburgh for reading and commenting on certain chapters which interested them. Finally, I would like to thank Katie Worrall of Darton, Longman and Todd for her interest in and encouragement of the project.

ROBERT CRAWFORD

ONE

The Breaking Point

Recently a tax inspector was hauled to safety after dangling from a window sixty feet above the ground. He intended suicide, and kept shouting to be allowed to die as his colleagues dragged him from the window ledge. We don't usually think of tax inspectors in this way; we are more likely to judge that his victims might try to commit such an act! We are advised, particularly if we have heart trouble, to read our tax claim lying down, not standing up! But did the tax inspector's colleagues have the right to interfere? Is suicide not legal? Have we not the moral right to end our lives if we consider them worthless? Why should people try to stop us? Is this not a free society?

These and other questions will occupy our attention in this chapter and the next one, and we will try to glean insights from both philosophy and religion. Apart from the person's right to die, we will be asking if there is a difference between taking one's life and giving it, and how difficult it is to exercise proper judgement concerning the act of suicide.

REASONS FOR SUICIDE

The list is endless: depression, loneliness, failure in business or marriage, anger, despair, incurable disease, revenge . . . Signs of a potential suicide are loss of interest in work, loss of appetite, self-reproach, decline in sexual interest and insomnia.[1] But these signs are not always obvious. I remember a colleague coming to see me about some simple matter. We had an amicable conversation in my office. There was nothing to indicate that he was in distress, apart from some grumbles about the administration in our college. I had seen a lot more anger in other colleagues on this subject, so I did not treat it as something out of the ordinary. But what he did the next day was extraordinary: he leapt off the cliff at Beachy Head near Eastbourne. Obviously there were a lot more things causing the depression than worries about the administration, but they were 'masked'. Doctors admit that they can be fooled by patients who come to them with physical complaints but who are really suffering from stress. The prescribing of sedatives can help a little, but often the patient becomes more incapacitated and decides that he does not want to continue living.

There is usually a mixture of reasons or patterns at work, and it is difficult to isolate even one or two. For example, how are we to view the suicide of the poet Sylvia Plath, estranged wife of poet Ted Hughes, on 11 February 1963? Aged 30, she killed herself in her London flat. One view is that she had been driven to death by a selfish, oppressive husband and the responsibility of motherhood. Ted Hughes had left her for another woman, and she had nursed griev-ances against her father, long dead, who had betrayed her by dying when she was very young. A contrary view of this complex woman has appeared in a biography. It reveals her as a disturbed and unpleasant woman; possessive, vindictive and hysterical. She forced Hughes, a patient, long-suffering man, to do his writing in almost impossible conditions. When she got into uncontrollable rages she even destroyed his manuscripts. Which viewpoint is correct? The emergence of a literature which attempts to answer this question shows how difficult it is to make a judgement.

British society, with its high unemployment rate, has produced an upward trend in parasuicide (a non-fatal attempt) and suicide. The incidence of parasuicide is ten times higher among the unemployed than among the employed, and the longer the period of unemployment, the higher the risk.[2] In the USA more individuals die as a result of suicide than homicide, with depression as the main cause. Has this a genetic cause? Scientists are discovering genes for depression, violence, alcoholism, homosexuality and suicide. Thus, for example, the criminal can now argue: 'Don't blame me, my actions were predetermined by chemicals in my brain.' Before his trial genetic tests might be made and and a replacement of the defective gene suggested. Embryos could also be tested and a decision made whether or not to abort on the basis of the quality of the genes. We cannot get into this fascinating discussion, but note that most researchers hold that we are made by nature and nurture and that genes predispose but do not determine what a person's behaviour will be.

Surprisingly, famous people have praised suicide, though it was illegal in this country until 1961. Immanuel Kant (1724–1804), the eminent philosopher, condemned suicide on the grounds that we must always act so that we can make our action into a universal rule, but he did recognise that there were conditions which permitted suicide. If a man was unjustly convicted of a crime and condemned to a life as a galley slave, we would not fault him if he chose death. Better to die than live as an object of contempt.

THE EFFECT OF SUICIDE ON OTHERS

The act usually makes us recoil in dismay, for life seems attractive to most of us. Doctors and nurses committed to saving life describe suicide in the hospital wards as an agonising and devastating experience which leaves a trail of angry feeling and despair. These feelings linger and depress them long after the event. A male nurse has graphically described his first experience of suicide. A young man tried to hang himself from a rail with a pyjama cord. Screaming filled the ward as the other patients witnessed the act. Somebody started artificial respiration and cardiac massage. Miraculously the heart-beat fluttered and the man gradually recovered. After such incidents, especially when they result in death, there is an inquest and always the fear that the nursing staff will be blamed. For years afterwards the male nurse used to wake in the night agonising: 'Did I miss something? Did I make a mistake? Was it my fault?' The effort of coping with the management's concern for the correct procedures rather than staff feelings and with relatives accusing them of neglect has resulted in many nurses leaving the profession.[3]

Some writers argue that suicide is morally neutral, for morality is concerned about relations with other people. But the effect of suicide on hospital staff, relatives and society must not be underestimated.

IS SUICIDE EVER JUSTIFIED?

In the past it has been both defended and condemned. The ancient Greeks tolerated suicide, though some of their

4

philosophers opposed it on the basis that it was cowardly and an injustice against the state. Plato rejected it because a man is a soldier of God and must stay at his post until God calls. Eminent Romans killed themselves, but for honourable reasons, such as setting an example of courage to their followers. Slaves and soldiers were forbidden to commit suicide, for masters could ill afford to lose their slaves and the state its soldiers.

In Greece, suicide was eventually approved by the state. Moreover, a supply of poison was kept by the magistrates for those who wished to die. The only requirement was that reasons for the act must be submitted, such as a hatred of life or a feeling of being overwhelmed by fate or grief. Stoicism, which accepted life with fortitude and to some extent with contempt, argued that we should not be moved either by good news or bad. We should leave the world 'as one might leave a smokey room'. Some of the extreme Stoics chose death rather than the pain of an injured finger or a gumboil! But in general philosophy maintained that the suicidal act should be rational. Taking one's life instead of undergoing torture or because of an incurable disease would be worthy of admiration.

Christianity in the second and third centuries insisted that anyone who took his life should be refused a Christian burial and that his goods and property should be confiscated by the state.[4] Life had been given by God, and only he had the right to take it. Jerome, in the fourth century, said that suicide was justified in defence of virginity, but Augustine rejected such a concession, contending that rape could not violate the soul's chastity. Church councils from the fifth century onwards denied funeral rites to suicides and threatened excommunication. In the thirteenth century Thomas Aquinas contended that suicide left no time for repentance and was a sin against nature, charity, society and God. It violated God's rights, just as a disobedient slave injured the rights of his master. It opposed the community's rights by depriving it of one of its parts, and it offended against the love that a person should have toward himself.

But the question may be raised at this point: Is this attitude to suicide in line with scriptural teaching? We must look more closely at Scripture to see if it is. There are a number of suicides in the Old Testament. Abimelech, one of the judges of Israel, was injured by a millstone dropped by a woman from a tower. It was considered a disgrace for a man to be killed by a woman, so the injured Abimelech called upon his servant to kill him (Judges 9:54). It was assisted suicide. In the case of Saul, his servant refused to help, so (according to one version) he killed himself by falling on his sword (1 Samuel 31:4). But, according to another version, a foreigner killed him. And when Ahithophel, advisor to both David and Absalom, had his advice rejected, he went and hanged himself (2 Samuel 17:23). But the most famous case is that of Samson, who brought down a temple upon himself and the Philistines (Judges 16:30). Since we will see motive and intention as important in considering the act of suicide, we may ask why and for what purpose these acts were performed. Abimelech did not want to be remembered as one who had been killed by a woman; Saul feared what the Philistines would do to him, remembering how they had blinded Samson when he had fallen into their hands; and Ahithophel was convinced when Absalom did not take his advice that the rebellion against David would fail and he would be found guilty of treason as a conspirator. Some commentators have seen these acts as selfish, but it seems that they are more in accord with the Greek and Roman attitudes – namely, choosing death rather than dishonour.

Samson's motivation was revenge; we can see this in the prayer he prayed before destroying his enemies. His suicide is not condemned by Scripture itself. It could be thought of as an act of war and part of his lifetime fight against the Philistines. Interestingly, Augustine, whom we recall opposed suicide, in the case of Samson made an exception. He put forward the concept of a just war; Samson, he argued, was engaged in such a war against the Philistines, since they opposed the authority of God. Samson, then, was under the direct control of the Spirit of God when he pulled down the temple,[5] and according to the New Testament he was a hero (Hebrews 11:32).

In the Gospels there is the infamous case of Judas' betrayal of Jesus and subsequent suicide. Apparently, he committed suicide because of remorse (Matthew 27:3). The Greek word translated as 'remorse' in some versions really means to change one's mind and purpose. Why did Judas change his mind? Did he see that the betrayal of a friend for money was sinful? If he was a calculating man and held the position of treasurer in the disciple band, why did he do an impetuous and irrational act which would result in such regret? Perhaps his motive was not money but an attempt to put Jesus into a position where he would have to use his power to escape. Certainly the disciples did not seem to know the difference between the materialistic kingdom which they wanted and the spiritual one which Jesus taught. The crowds, too, on one occasion tried to make Jesus a king by force. Judas perhaps thought that when Jesus was put to the test he would set up the kind of kingdom the Jews wanted. These and other speculations surround the person of Judas, but he remains both in motive and intention the 'mystery man' of the Gospels. What is condemned, however, is not his suicide but the betrayal of

Jesus, which is seen as the work of the devil (Luke 22:3; John 13:27).

The case of Judas does say something to those who have reached the breaking point of utter despair. He felt that his position was hopeless, but Peter, who had denied Christ, found repentance. It could be argued, however, that denial was just as bad as betrayal. Perhaps the greatest mistake of Judas was to place a limit on the grace of God.

Our survey of biblical evidence indicates that there was no general condemnation of suicide. However, as with other matters, we cannot say that such silence meant consent. Since the early followers of Jesus were Jews and Judaism condemned suicide, the writers of the New Testament may have thought that there was no need to mention such condemnation.[6] Later writers did condemn because they saw some Christians actively pursuing death in order to gain the martyr's crown; they argued that Christians should face up to persecution and not flee from it by suicidal means. Later still Augustine and Aquinas finalised the arguments against suicide. However, the period of the Renaissance, with its stress on individualism, humanism and the recovery of Greek and Roman ideas, paved the way for a more liberal attitude to suicide.

The Christian writer John Donne (1573–1631), Dean of St Paul's, defended suicide. He argued that while self-preservation is a general principle there may be times when awful conditions force a person to think of suicide. Such an act is not politically or socially harmful unless it is cowardly or a retreat from duties. It is not against the law of God, especially if it benefits humankind.

However, it was the philosopher David Hume (1711–1776) who contended most strongly for the liberty of the individual in this matter. He said that there was no Scripture that actually forbade it and that the proper translation of the sixth commandment was 'Thou shalt not murder', murder being the killing of another human being.

But there is one verse in Scripture against suicide: 'For your life blood I will surely require a reckoning' (Genesis 9:5). The Jewish rabbis often quoted it. Yet it is strange that there is no mention of it with regard to the scriptural suicide cases which we have looked at. What we do note is that these people in their lives had earned the disapproval of God and that the same kind of atmosphere attends the end of their lives. Hume's argument develops in the context of the government of God and our relation to society. God, he argues, governs the world by his laws, but within them he leaves liberty for us so that we are free to dispose of our lives if we reason that this is in our best interest and for the general good. If someone feels that his life has become a burden it is courageous and wise of him to dispense with it. Hume opened up the way for utilitarian arguments that one should act on the basis of whether one's action will bring benefit to society. These arguments tended to make suicide a social rather than a religious concern.

Hume's arguments rest on what is called natural religion, which sees God governing the world by immutable laws and not interfering with them. He does not leave room for what is called revealed religion, in which God acts to bring about change and put things right. An example of this is the Christian belief in the incarnation of God. Suicide, Hume contends, is not intrinsically wrong but should be judged with reference to others. This ignores considerations about the character of the person concerned and about motives and intentions that might have prompted her suicide and that generally could be held to have a bearing on the moral quality of the action.[7]

Hume was drawing attention to two principles that were to be influential in subsequent discussion of ethical issues.

The first was a person's right to make a choice, and the second was the idea that an action should be examined to see if it produced consequences that benefited others. These are called the principles of autonomy and utility, and they are often in tension with a third principle which has been stressed by Christianity and other religions: the sanctity of life. Hume's second principle opened up the way for utilitarianism, which has an effect on our decision-making today. According to this philosophy the result of an action is morally crucial, and we should aim at those actions which bring the greatest happiness to the greatest number of people. It was expounded by Jeremy Bentham (1784–1832) and John Stuart Mill (1806–1873).

Utilitarianism is very attractive, since we naturally seek happiness and try to avoid pain. Bentham stressed that self-interest is predominant over 'social interest' and that a person only sacrifices his self-interest when he is connected with someone by 'the narrow tie of sympathy'. But this self-interest conflicts with the principle of the 'greatest happiness of the greatest number'. It would appear then that if a person thought suicide was in his best interest, and if it would not break the tie of sympathy with others, it would be all right. It is recorded that in his dying moments Bentham requested to be assisted to die.

For Mill too the rightness or wrongness of an action depended on its consequences, and he tried to avoid the problem of each person seeking her own happiness by stressing the welfare of the community. He pointed out that if a child was rewarded when she did something that benefited people she would experience pleasure and would think that making others happy increased her own happiness. Education was necessary if utilitarianism was to be properly understood. This applied to the principle of autonomy or personal freedom. I should not interfere with another person unless I thought she was going to do harm to other people. Our natural instinct if we see a man or woman standing on Beachy Head with their body close to the edge is to shout and warn of the danger, and if we think they are going to jump we rush to prevent this. Why? Because we think that life is valuable and not to be thrown away. This is the principle of the sanctity of life. However, Mill held that 'over his own body and mind, the individual is sovereign'. The principle of the sanctity of life can come into conflict with the greatest happiness principle, since sometimes it is necessary to let some people die in order that the many shall live. But did Mill then advocate suicide? Not directly, but there are pointers that way in his writings. He recognises that what we do could hurt others, and as we are members of a society this is very difficult to avoid. But his definition of liberty is 'doing what one desires'. What, then, if I desire to commit suicide? According to Mill we should give warning if we see someone standing too near the edge of a cliff but not do anything else if we are certain that the person knows the risk she is taking. Diane Collinson comments:

> Mill's account of individual liberty provides little scope for justifying intervention. Even if one is of the opinion that most people who embark on suicide do so irrationally, it follows from his view that once it is known that a prospective suicide is adult, rational and self-commanding in the ways specified by Mill, intervention should cease or should not be attempted.[8]

Modern utilitarians place the emphasis on the individual's right to decide if his life in the future would be worthwhile and if an act of suicide would hurt other people. Both are difficult to decide, since there is need to establish what a worthwhile life is, and his view of what hurting others is may be different from theirs. A problem arises from any philosophy which pays attention to the consequences and results of actions while giving insufficient consideration to motives and intentions. This was the view of Immanuel Kant, who realised that the inner springs of action should be taken into account. Actions should not be based on inclination or wants or desires or fear or feeling but on duty. This rules out suicide motivated by cowardice or lack of regard for our obligations. Kant is generally against suicide, for how could we make it into a universal rule? However, there could be exceptional cases. He cites the eminent Roman, Cato, who rather than fall into the hands of Caesar committed suicide. He would not submit to Caesar, for he knew that if he did other Romans could follow his example. So he chose death in order to inspire them to resistance. Suicide in this case, according to Kant, is a virtue. But this concession on his part suggests that he was slipping into utilitarianism, for Cato chose death because of its effect on Roman society.

The emphasis on the experience of the individual and his freedom to choose reached its height in the philosophy of existentialism. An illustration leads us into this way of thinking. Imagine a young man called Mathieu leaning over the parapet of a bridge and looking down into the cold waters below. Suddenly he realises the extent of his freedom to commit suicide. Life lacks meaning, he feels isolated and desolate, anguish grips his mind. 'I'm going to kill myself,' he cries, but then without any apparent reason he decides not to do it and thinks, 'Next time, perhaps.'[9]

This picture painted by Jean Paul Sartre (1905–1980) shows us some of the essentials of existentialism. The young man on the bridge is reduced to *angst*, which is the anguished dread present in all human beings. Individualism here reaches its full flower with the stress on the inner world of the person. It is we who make ourselves, not our nature or environment or rules. What we know about ourselves is that we exist, and all that we can say about our mental and physical constitution is that we have certain qualities or capacities. These do not determine our actions; we are free to choose, and this brings with it tremendous responsibility. In a crisis situation such as suicide we do not bring ready-made external values but create our own. Existentialism emphasises the self and personal experience. Mathieu in Sartre's illustration realises that he has the freedom to commit suicide, for he is a human being and not a thing. Suicide is the ultimate challenge to his freedom, for it will end his freedom. The responsibility of such freedom is terrifying.

Sartre appears to believe that if I commit suicide I remove meaning from my life because by ending it I destroy the possibility of subsequently giving meaning to the act. Existentialism is asserting that we are responsible and cannot shift that responsibility to others. Thus in the case of suicide, one would be burdening someone else with the responsibility of explaining to others what the meaning of the act was! This appears to imply that suicide is ruled out by Sartre, but there may be cases where it could be undertaken in good faith.

We shall return to existentialism again in the course of this book. It has value in stressing the freedom and responsibility of the individual, though it neglects the social character of morality and the influence of tradition upon us. We do not make values out of nothing. But this philosophy does what utilitarianism fails to do – it emphasises the inner life of the person and her value over against the happiness and demands of the community.

Christian thinkers are attracted by certain aspects of existentialism – such as its stress on the value of the individual and his freedom, and its analysis of the plight of human-kind. But Christianity is more than an individualistic ethic; it is concerned with the person in the community, and involves taking other people seriously:

> To do this is to try to look at situations and problems through the eyes of the people involved. We need only to consider the possible benefits of a worker seeing with management eyes and vice versa to realise the importance of 'putting ourselves in the other person's shoes'. To consider the problem from someone else's viewpoint means that we cannot simply please our-selves without reference to the wishes and desires of others. It is not easy to see things from another perspec-tive especially if we are in initial disagreement with that person. Yet the effort is worthwhile if we are to make a fully informed moral decision.[10]

This, as we have seen, is very important in thinking about the act of suicide.

TAKING LIFE OR GIVING IT

We have seen that some acts of suicide are viewed differ-ently from others. We need to look more closely at the kind of act which could be considered sacrificial rather than a self-killing which desires death for its own sake. In the history of the Jews there is the famous case of Masada, a fortress besieged by the Romans. With defeat staring them in the face, the defenders were addressed by their leader: 'There is still', he said, 'the free choice of noble death . . . Let our wives die thus undishonoured . . . Men will testify that we preferred death to slavery . . . It is death which gives liberty to the soul and permits it to depart free from all calamity . . . Unenslaved by the foe, let us die as free men; with our children and wives let us quit this life together.' Of the 960 people in the fortress, all killed themselves except two women and five children.[11]

The motive was to escape slavery and the intention was to gain an honourable death. No selfish reasons or cowardice were involved. The Jews have highly honoured them until this day. This is the giving of life for a noble aim, whereas the term 'suicide' could be reserved for the seeking of death itself with no larger intention in mind. In the same way, the Charge of the Light Brigade and Captain Oates' walking out into the snow during Scott's Antarctic expedition are seen as sacrifices. Men who have starved themselves to death for patriotic reasons, the martyrs of the Christian Church and those who gave their lives in the two World Wars are also seen as having died sacrificially. Yet controversy surrounds these acts. Did the Light Brigade need to charge? Were the IRA men who starved themselves to death to be regarded as martyrs? The Roman Catholic Church refused to condemn their act on the grounds that it was done for a cause larger than themselves.[12] With regard to the First World War, we still hear criticisms of the inept military leadership which led to such a waste of life. The soldiers were 'lions led by donkeys'. The debate continues.

Apart from motive and intention, there is the act itself. A lot depends on its passive or active nature. A suicide may be called passive when the person does not intentionally seek death for its own sake as a benefit for himself but rather seeks it in order to benefit others or for the sake of a higher cause. Thus the verdict of the Catholic Church on the IRA hunger strikers. But in the history of the Church there were those who, because they wanted either to escape persecution or to gain the glory of martyrdom, actively sought death. This was not acceptable to the Church.

Is there a difference, then, between a patient in hospital who refuses treatment which will save his life and a person who shoots himself? The problem becomes even more difficult if we look upon refusing as an act. This will need some attention in our next chapter.

Many acts which we view as sacrifice do contain the active element. Captain Oates *walked* out of the tent and Socrates *drank* the hemlock.[13] Oates did not directly kill himself; it was the blizzard that killed him but he did knowingly put himself in a position where he could not survive. It is most difficult to get at this inner spring of action, and we can only surmise the many thoughts that must have passed through the mind of Oates as he surveyed the desperate position that he and his friends were experiencing. While he may have had a number of reasons for deliberately walking out into the snow, one of them must have been by his departure to give his friends some hope of surviving. He could not think of any other way of doing this, and so he was prepared to make the sacrifice. The act had a utilitarian basis, for it looked to the consequence – the saving of his friends – and this would mean (or so he thought) their happiness. But it is difficult to forecast the result of any action. Aware of this, Utilitarians sometimes speak of acting on the basis of probable consequences. In the case of Oates, his act, though well intended, did not save his friends, for the entire expedition perished a few days later.

At this point we may be despairing of finding a case free from all the difficulties that philosophers can raise! But let us imagine a Jewish patriot who penetrates the Syrian lines as a spy during the war between Israel and Syria. He becomes trusted by the Syrians, sends valuable information home and eventually returns himself. But there is more information which they need. However, his chief warns him that it could be suicide to go back because by now the Syrians will suspect that there is a spy in their midst. But though he knows the risk he is confident that they will not catch him. In the event they do and he takes cyanide pills.

Is it suicide or sacrifice? The motive, love of his country, was good, and the intention, victory for his people, was a worthy one. He knew that torture awaited him if he did not take the pills. He did not seek death; there was no other way. He took the pills only because he wanted to be in a condition in which he could not be forced by torture to reveal information which was vital to his country. His capture took him by surprise, and indeed there was always the possibility that he might have escaped detection. His chief had warned him of the possibility of capture, but it had never been a certainty. If it is argued that he put himself in a position where death might ensue, it could be countered that the life itself is a risk and that many people are killed every day in normal circumstances. Kant would accept the Israeli's act as choosing death rather than violating duty to his country. But while it was something which circumstances forced him to do, it was a direct self-killing, not an indirect one. Killing, of course, is bad, but generally it has been accepted and even praised when the aim has been a good one.

THE DIFFICULTY OF JUDGEMENT

No case requires more sympathy than that of suicide, for there is such a mixture of motive, intention and consequence that various judgements can be made. Let us start with a definition: Suicide takes place when a person intentionally brings about her death, is not coerced to do so and arranges the conditions of it for herself.[14] The IRA hunger strikers arranged the conditions of their death, so by this definition their act was indeed suicide, despite the verdict pronounced by the Catholic Church. But a definition which left out the words 'and arranges the conditions' could allow the Catholic verdict! Even with the usual reasons for suicide we can think of different judgements.

Strong arguments can be mounted against the sort of view which sees suicide as cowardice or a crime against society or nature or God or human dignity. To say it is cowardly is to ignore the bravery required to do it. To say it is against society is to forget the utilitarian argument that it sometimes benefits society. To say it is against the natural desire for life is to fail to remember how difficult life can be. To say it is against God requires stronger evidence from the Bible than we have got. To affirm that it is against self-respect is to fail to take into account cases of steady decline of mental and physical disability in which the sufferer is prevented from dying with dignity.[15]

On the other side of the coin there is the principle of the sanctity of life as stated in the commandment 'Thou shalt not kill'. But it is agreed that 'kill' here means 'murder'. Since the Israelites themselves killed both in war and capital punishment the way is open for someone to argue that if killing is sometimes right, then suicide is right. What is the difference between killing yourself and killing someone else who is not innocent? Soldiers kill the enemy who has demonstrated his lack of innocence by killing innocent people in his trail of conquest. Thus the principle of the sanctity of life is modified to become an argument against the killing of innocent people. But the parallel between self-killing and killing other innocent people breaks down, since I am depriving the latter of the life which belongs to them. However, the suicide sometimes finds that he is not innocent, as in the case of Judas. Of course, if I take the position that life is sacred because it is God-given, then I cannot dispose of it. This, as we have seen, figures prominently in Christian arguments.

THE CHURCHES

The Church of England accepts most of the arguments against viewing suicide as morally blameworthy which we have mentioned and points out that developments in psychology show that not many suicides today are wholly voluntary and deliberate. Further, it recognises that human behaviour is far more complex than it at first appears. Hence the Church does not condemn suicides which are involuntary – for example, those which are forced by torture or threat of rape or those which follow mental derangement.

But the Church of England condemns suicides which are voluntary and selfish, for they substitute the human power to end life for the power of Christ. Human beings acknowledge the victory of death whereas the Christian believes that Christ has overcome this last enemy. Thus the death of a suicide as an end in itself is not acceptable. If, however, suicide is hardly distinguishable from self-sacrifice in that life is given for something greater than itself, then it is justifiable. Heroic deaths like that of Captain Oates fall into this category, as do the deaths of martyrs, certain ascetics and possibly the chronic invalid who kills himself to relieve his family and society of an impossible burden. Significantly, the Church of England broadly accepts the utilitarian argument that the legitimacy of suicide depends on the benefit which it brings to others. In reply to the argument that killing is justified in the case of war and perhaps as a punishment for murder, the Church makes the point that no easy parallelism between these two cases and suicide can be made, since both in war and capital punishment the decision to kill is a corporate one. With regard to the question of self-killing precluding repentance, which the Church traditionally used as an argument against suicide, the Church of England envisages the 'larger hope' remarking, 'for who would say what opportunities God in his mercy and love may or may not provide after death?'[16]

It would seem that, with some modifications, the other Protestant Churches would agree. But the Catholic Church takes a strong stand against suicide and will only consider it morally possible in certain circumstances, as in the case of the hunger strikers. In 1980 the Vatican's Declaration on Euthanasia referred to suicide as murder. It is a rejection of God's sovereignty, a denial of love, of self-respect and of the natural instinct to live.

However, the Catholic Church does recognise that there can be psychological factors present which diminish responsibility or even remove it. The Church affirms that 'one must clearly distinguish suicide from that sacrifice of one's life whereby for a higher cause, such as God's glory, the salvation of souls or the service of one's brethren, a person offers his or her own life or puts it in danger'.[17]

WHAT ABOUT THE LAW?

Suicide or attempted suicide was a criminal offence in England until the Act of Parliament in 1961, and assisted suicide continues to be a crime. Today there is increasing emphasis placed upon 'intention' in the act, and many verdicts of accident rather than suicide are recorded. This results, as we have seen, from the difficulty of determining what was actually going on in the person's mind when the act occurred. In America some states have repealed the laws against suicide, while others have not. Philosophers contend that the US law has never addressed the issue properly, for while the Constitution protects the right of self-determination in many matters of personal choice, including how the body is treated, it also recognises state interference in preventing suicide. Some argue that the Supreme Court would need to make clear the principle determining personal choices and to stipulate which are protected from state interference and which are not. Philosophers argue for suicide on the grounds of rational choice and competency and think that the Court should state these.[18]

Suicide is intentional self-killing, as we have noted. But a person in hospital may refuse treatment, not intending to die, but believing perhaps that she does not need it or that some other agency such as God will effect her cure. Thus Jehovah's Witnesses have refused blood transfusions and Christian Scientists surgery. The case of a patient suffering from an incurable disease and from whom it has been decided to withhold treatment is quite different from that of a healthy, rational person who makes the choice of ending his life. And it is this choice which the philosophers in question want to be recognised.

THE RIGHT TO DIE

Some people in their approach to the problem of suicide concentrate on the principle of autonomy or self-rule. The word 'autonomy' has Greek origins (*autos* = 'self'; *nomos* = 'law') and it implies free choice, rights, responsibility, and the creating of values. These, as we have seen, feature in various ways in the philosophy of existentialism, but we have maintained that morality concerns persons in society and that for this reason rights are limited. This will apply to a lot of things – for example, to the right of free speech. It is limited to truth telling, so if I scandalise someone I may be prosecuted for it. For each individual to have rights without limitations would injure others. Moreover, unlimited behaviour could set a bad example.

As we will see in the next chapter, many harrowing cases can be presented of patients in hospital or at home wanting to die and seeking assistance from doctors and relatives. These individuals may seem rational. Are we opposing their right to die? Interference is of course allowed in the cases of the immature and the mentally incompetent. But a survey of law cases in the United States shows how difficult it is to define the words, 'rational' and 'competent'. Some attempted definitions have stipulated that the individual must have sufficient information to make a decision, no signs that there is a pessimistic frame of mind and freedom from coercive pressures or influences. Indeed, pure rationality may be an ideal. Even if we discard the evidence which indicates that most suicides are irrational, we have to admit that we do act 'out of character' at times. This could be devastating in a life and death issue.

It is probably true that our society is interfering less and less with individual choice and decision, and there seem to be cases where people know that someone is likely to commit suicide but do nothing to help. This could indicate an uncaring society. At the same time, my right to die must be placed over and against the fact that my death may injure others. What we need to achieve, difficult though it is, is a balance between respect for the person's autonomy and the right of the state to intervene to prevent an individual from doing harm to himself.

A number of studies have been made of attempted suicides. One undertaken in Edinburgh examined the cases of a large number of individuals who made serious suicide bids. The follow-up showed that only 29 per cent went on to take their lives later. The British Medical Association Report on Euthanasia makes a relevant comment on this:

'It seems that there is strong reason to act so as to save or preserve life even where the individual concerned has avowed or indicated by his deeds that he wishes to die.'[19] We will look again at the rights of the individual in succeeding chapters.

It has been suggested by philosophers that to try and understand suicide in terms of rights, obligations and duties is to miss the real question, which is this: Is suicide the kind of thing a good person would do? This is an interesting proposal, but the difficulty here is the pluralistic nature of modern society, in which there is little consensus about what good is. The Old Testament describes a community in which 'every man did what was right in his own eyes' (Judges 17:6; 21:25), since there was no central authority. While we are not quite in that situation, we do have this continual tension between what the individual considers to be right and what the state sees as right. There are people who do not live up to the values of society and there are others who will not live down to them! Both attitudes may lead to suicide.

CONCLUSION

Albert Camus (1913–1960) was convinced that suicide was a judgement on life: 'There is but one truly serious philosophical problem and that is suicide. Judging whether life is or is not worth living amounts to answering the fundamental question of philosophy.'[20] Perhaps there are more problems and tensions today than there were in the past; as a result more people reach 'the point of no return' and want to end it all. In thinking about such an act they will, if rational, consider many factors, such as their freedom to choose between life and death; whether their death will benefit others; whether they have the strength and will to continue; whether there is any purpose left in life and whether they can handle their suffering... If these reflections do lead them to choose death, the act still comes as a shock to us, for one of our main drives is self-preservation, and to go against this requires not only courage but the conclusion that life is meaningless. One needs to have sympathy and understanding in order to be able to stand in this person's shoes and see why she committed suicide.

The decision to end one's life is not made on the basis of nothing, as the existentialist seems to be saying, but in the context of an understanding of life. Christianity, traditionally, provided a framework of meaning in the Western world. Christians, inspired by the courage of the people of the early Church, who despite terrible suffering patiently endured, found meaning in their lives. Today, while secular society rejects this framework, it does admit that countries where Christianity and Islam predominate have a lower rate of suicide. Sociologists, in examining this trend, point to Arabic countries where Islam is the dominant religion and to places such as Latin America and Ireland where Catholicism plays a leading role. It is true that Ireland shows an increase in suicide rates, but this could be due to the increasing secularisation of the country which has taken place in recent years. We have to be careful about such statistics, since other factors are involved and there is no generally accepted theory to explain such differences between countries. However, this is certainly a subject that merits more research.[21]

Philosophers who do not accept this religious framework in its doctrinal aspects do agree that our lives are not just like a piece of property that we can dispose of when we feel like it. David Lamb says: 'Life is not a property: it is the capacity to have experiences which can neither be bought or sold. Perhaps certain experiences can be purchased but life which is the state in which experiences take place, is not a disposable commodity.'[22] The taking of life, even in the face of awful suffering, is such a responsibility that it can only be a last resort when every other avenue has been explored. What is needed in our society is more caring agencies that will be at hand in such a crisis of life and able to put the person going through this crisis in touch with others who have had a similar experience.[23]

For those who reject the religious framework there is the possibility of considering carefully how meaning can be found within life itself. This is a naturalism which stresses the ethical virtues of love, justice, courage, loyalty and humility. It reflects on human nature, the mystery of the source of everything and the transience of earthly life. Through this reflection the individual seeks to preserve his life.[24] We shall consider this again in our final chapter.

If moral difficulties enter into the act of suicide which, though it has social implications is very personal, we may expect even greater problems when asking someone to assist us to die. These we discuss in our next chapter.

Questions for discussion
- What do you think is the main cause of suicide?
- If a hunger striker dies as a consequence of his or her hunger strike is that death a suicide?
- Suppose a suicide affects no one but the person killed. Can there be any moral objection to it?
- The Church has traditionally opposed suicide. Do you think it was right?
- Is the question of suicide relative to different cultures so, for example, in Japanese culture Hara Kiri is regarded as honourable, a way of putting it all right?

TWO

A Good Death

Sara Johnson, an intelligent and athletic girl, took an overdose of sleeping pills because she was suffering from multiple sclerosis, which causes a steady deterioration of the mind and of the muscles of the body. She had to be washed and lifted in and out of bed by her mother and her nurses, and couldn't even feed herself. She tried to write a book entitled *How I Beat MS*, but gradually, as the disease tightened its grip upon her, she gave up and took an overdose.

Her parents had entered into a pact with her, promising that they would not intervene if she decided to end her life. When she took the lethal mixture of drugs they sat by her bedside and watched her die. She left a message on her personal computer: 'Dear everyone, this is the hardest letter I have ever had to write. I just wanted to say that the MS and the psychiatric problems have reached a point at which I cannot bear. At least now you know that I am at peace, forgive me, lots of love, Sara.'

Did the Johnsons assist their daughter to die? The prosecution claimed that she could not have taken the tablets unaided, and three empty pill bottles were found in the kitchen with their tops screwed on. The defence admitted that there was a dispute about the background of the death but argued that the parents did not take any positive steps to end Sara's life and that their promise not to seek medical assistance had given her comfort. The judge said, 'Your failure to intervene was in keeping with the promise you made to her. Today you have acknowledged that it was contrary to the law, whatever the moral or ethical considerations involved. It is clear that you will benefit greatly from counselling and support.' They were given one year's probation.

The case raises the question of euthanasia or assisted suicide. The judge ruled that positive steps to end Sara's life could not be established and concluded that it was a case of 'letting die', which is often called passive euthanasia. In startling contrast there was the case of Frank C. Roberts in the United States who, convicted of the murder of his wife, was sentenced to life imprisonment. Yet the circumstances were not dissimilar. Roberts appeared to be a very devoted husband who could not stand to see his wife suffering from the same disease as Sara Johnson. She wished to die and not only had told friends of this desire but had made an unsuccessful attempt to kill herself. One night, with her body writhing in pain, she pleaded with her husband to fill a glass with poison and leave it at her bedside. He did so. When the case came to court the judge told him that it did not matter whether she had the intention of committing suicide or not; he had committed murder, which was an inhumane act. Despite the question of whether allowing her to continue suffering might have been more inhumane than assisting her to die, the Supreme Court of Michigan dismissed the appeal against the sentence.

Both were cases of euthanasia, a term which means 'a gentle and easy death'. In the case of the Johnsons it is called 'passive' since, because of the agreement which had been made, they did nothing to save their daughter. In hospital a doctor may decide not to prolong life, or he may make a non-treatment decision. But in the Roberts' case the euthanasia was judged to be 'active', done with the intention of terminating a life. The judge recognised that Mrs Roberts may have requested it, so we can call this case as well as that of Sara Johnson 'voluntary euthanasia'.

If Sara or Roberts' wife had not wanted to die, but it had been judged by the parents or Roberts that it would be better for them, these cases would have been instances of 'involuntary euthanasia'. This is the killing of someone who could consent but does not. The motive that is usually put forward is that death is in the sufferer's best interest. To further complicate matters there is what is called 'non-voluntary euthanasia'. If Sara or Roberts' wife had been in a permanent coma or mentally ill to a severe extent, then on a non-voluntary basis their lives might have been terminated.

In this chapter we shall be considering the arguments for and against all forms of euthanasia. We shall also look at the practice and reports of the Medical Association, active and passive euthanasia, the important matter of intention, the legal position, the teaching of the churches, the rights of patients and what is happening in Europe and America. But first of all we need to clarify our thoughts about what is meant by the term, 'death'.

THE END OF LIFE

When am I dead? I read that a surgeon can work inside the heart when there is no heartbeat and is able to keep the patient's brain alive by using a heart-lung machine. Is a person not dead when his heart stops? What about brain death? Are we moving from a clear definition of what death is to one that is more elusive and difficult? In October 1980 a BBC *Panorama* programme revealed that four patients in America who had been diagnosed as brain dead had subsequently recovered. It was said that this was due to transplant surgeons being in too big a hurry to get organs and failing to do the proper testing. Another American case was that of Karen Quinlan, who was taken to hospital with a loss of consciousness. She had only a sleepy awareness of what was going on around her. She was able to yawn, blink and cry out and would feel pain. Doctors put her on a respirator. Later, at her father's request, she was taken off, but to the surprise of the medical staff she was able to breathe without it. Her lower brain or brain stem had not died, and she continued to live in an unconscious state for many years.

The brain stem drives the heart, lungs etc., so death is often equated with it. But if a respirator is brought into use the patient may display reflex activity. Once the respirator stops the heart ceases to beat. If the brain stem is functioning properly then attention is paid to consciousness: the cerebral cortex. If she cannot be aroused she is in a coma. But if she is conscious though paralysed and unable to speak or swallow she is in a locked-in syndrome. Communication is by blinking or other eye movements. In these cases there is no withdrawal of life support. Thus it is what has happened to the brain and its distinctive functions that make life worthwhile and of ethical importance. Death will be certified on the basis of the irreversible cessation of cardiorespiratory function and the permanent functional end of the brain stem.

It is difficult to decide if the vegetative state is permanent or not but if it is agreed that there can be no ultimate hope for the patient it is argued that life should be terminated directly: active euthanasia. We will consider arguments for and against this procedure.

THE CASE FOR EUTHANASIA

In a TV programme a wife told of the suffering of her husband and his sincere desire to end his life. But he did not want to incriminate her in an assisted suicide. A husband related a similar story and admitted that he had helped his wife to die. They, and an Aids sufferer, spoke about the difficulty of committing suicide unaided and the loneliness of such a death. They pointed out that it would be better if the family doctor could be present to administer a fatal dosage in the presence of friends and relatives, so that the sufferer's last moments would be eased by their presence.

There are many old people who are no longer mentally competent and display various signs of distress and unhappiness. Some lack control of their bodily functions and are a problem to their relatives. Others suffer in hospital, having to tolerate tubes, drips and surgical wounds, controlled by doctors and nurses who apparently do not want to admit defeat. Why should people not be allowed to die with dignity?

What is the use of prolonging an existence which is full of pain and distress when death could release? On a utilitarian basis, the death would bring relief to the sufferer and benefit to the relatives. Some people, not wanting to be a burden, have drawn up 'living wills' which ask that they may be killed painlessly when their condition has deteriorated. A person has the right not to waste away. If suicide is legal, why should assisted suicide not be allowable? There is no comparison between a killing motivated by hatred or jealousy or revenge and a 'mercy killing' which is an act of love and compassion for a person in pain. In the Netherlands a physician who measures up to strict criteria can give a lethal injection to a dying person who requests it. Can we not accept this? Moreover, can we not accept a mercy killing where the request cannot be made – for example, in the case of a deformed child or a mentally incompetent old person?

The price of keeping people alive in hospital is enormous. First, their beds could be occupied by patients with a good chance of improvement. Second, there is the bad effect on the hospital staff involved, who have to watch them die slowly. Third, there is the suffering of the relatives, who had hoped that their loved ones would have a good and gentle end.

Should not respect for a person's autonomy mean that she not only has the right to die but should also be able to request the kind of treatment that she wants in hospital? But doctors do not always grant such requests and sometimes override them because, in their view, such treatment is not in the patient's interests. Is this not an infringement of rights? Doctors may also override the wishes of the relatives. Is this not giving them far too much power?

The BMA Report admits that doctors have given patients sedatives which if taken in quantity would kill and speaks of physicians 'who actively terminate the lives of certain patients at the behest of their own conscience and in secret'.[1] Would it not be better to legalise such a procedure? Controversy also surrounds some patients who are dependent on respirators. If such support were to be discontinued the patients would die. If a patient who is able to do so indicates that he wants the support to be withdrawn, the doctor is placed in a very difficult position, for such withdrawal means immediate death. But he will have to await a court's decision before he can act, since as the law stands it is impossible to maintain a hard and fast distinction between withdrawal of such support and assisted suicide. Would it not make life much easier for both patient and doctor if the law was already clear as to the proper procedure? If in the event the court decides he can withdraw the support, have they not agreed to assisted suicide in a particular case and therefore broken the existing law?

However, it could be contended that mercy killing would lead to killing for all sorts of reasons other than pain. The victims would be defective children, senior citizens (Romans advised relatives to throw them into the Tiber!) and mentally disabled people. But this is involuntary euthanasia, which is not being argued for. It resembles the elimination by the Nazis of those whom they saw as unfit to live in the Third Reich. If we concentrate on non-voluntary and voluntary euthanasia we are not likely to get side-tracked by the analogies drawn from Nazi Germany which are used by the 'slippery slope' opponents of euthanasia. Just as killing in self-defence happens in certain limited circumstances and has not led to murder, the option of dying with the assistance of a doctor or relative would not tend to produce widespread killing of those whom a society might consider useless. It must always be insisted that these forms of euthanasia are for the benefit of the sufferer and not meant to satisfy any racial or economic demands. Those who argue strongly against the killing of people who want to die or are in circumstances which prevent them from giving consent must produce the evidence that such mercy killing in other societies has led to involuntary euthanasia. The burden of proof lies with them.

In short, advocates of euthanasia base their arguments on the major claim that a person should have control over and choice about when, where and how he or she dies. This service should be provided by doctors; just as they seek to preserve life, they ought to be willing to end it when asked to do so.

ARGUMENTS AGAINST EUTHANASIA

Doctors do respect the wishes of their patients and only override them when they consider them to be contrary to reason. They seek to offer information about a course of treatment and why it should be undertaken or not. The overall assumption is that the patient respects the value of life and would want to live as long as possible. If the patient is unable to make a decision because of some incapacity the relatives will be consulted, but their motives will also need to be carefully assessed. In difficult cases other professionals will be consulted.

The principle of the sanctity of life is accepted by the doctor, and voluntary euthanasia runs counter to this principle. In some cases where sedatives have been given it has been found that patients have not used them. It was the fear of being the victim of terminal illness and of the helplessness that goes with it that led to requests. Of one person the BMA Report says: 'Once that fear was allayed she could die with peace and dignity and she was quite content to live out her remaining life with the assurance that her doctor would not abandon her.'[2]

If a doctor is 'compelled by conscience to intervene to end a person's life', then he must be prepared 'to face the closest scrutiny of this action that the law might wish to make'.[3] But doctors do not necessarily seek to prolong life when there is no point. 'Letting die' is acceptable. This will be discussed in more detail in a later section. Doctors insist that their refusal to accede to requests for death is often based on the knowledge that those requests are irrational. Duncan Vere, Professor of Therapeutics in the University of London, gives the example of a man who endured so much during two resuscitations that he requested to be allowed to die if cardiac arrest recurred. The arrest did recur, but he was revived by a passer-by who was unaware of his request. Two years later, Vere says, he was at the centre of a happy family, apparently in perfect health and having forgotten the distress of his resuscitation. Vere contends that the only patient of his who ever asked to be 'put to death' was clearly confused. He gave him a phenothiazine derivate. The following day the patient was more orientated and was sitting up by the window making remarks about the sunshine. He had forgotten all about his request to die! Vere concludes from such cases that judgement can be impaired by much suffering or the imagined prospect of it. While Vere's experience cannot be generalised, it does raise the question of how widespread requests to die are and suggests a need for caution in dealing with them.[4]

Stephen Hawking, the eminent physicist, is a surviving victim of motor neurone disease which usually kills within five years. He caught pneumonia and had to have a tracheotomy operation which removed his power of speech. His wife, faced with the decision to turn off his life-support machine, refused saying that her whole existence had been geared to keeping Stephen alive. The tracheotomy robbed him of the power of speech but he was provided with a computer-generated voicebox and though there is no cure for his condition he continues to make a remarkable contribution to our understanding of science. He said that the feeling of wanting to die only lasted a short time and that he is glad to be alive.

Those who argue for euthanasia say that it will not lead to involuntary acts of killing. But their opponents doubt this. They take the point that there is little danger of racial motives being involved, as happened with the Nazis, but are concerned about their opponents' stress on economic factors such as saving the cost of care and freeing hospital beds. Could we find ourselves on an economic slippery slope? How long would it be before we wondered if we could really afford the handicapped and the old? Is euthanasia not the last resort of an uncaring society? Killing on the part of doctors would add to the violence in the community.

The suffering of patients in hospital or at home can be relieved by drugs and only a small number require heavy sedation. Normally these patients do not ask for their lives to be taken.[5] For the terminally ill, care and understanding are just as important as drugs. This approach has been fully developed by the hospice. Those who administer such places contend that their patients do not desire to die, for an attempt is made to attend not only to their physical needs but also to their psychological and spiritual needs. There are now over a hundred independent and NHS hospices in this country in addition to many hospital support teams and home care services.

It is argued that palliative care provided in the UK is the best in the world and if other countries had it there would not be the desire for active euthanasia. Opponents argue that the approach is hypocritical since the doctors know that they are using drugs which shorten life. Supporters, however, of Cicely Saunders, the founder of the hospice, argue that she has changed the face of death of millions of people and she has been awarded many prizes for her work. She places stress on the holistic approach, a treating of the whole person, and is motivated by religious convictions. She argues that nobody need die in pain who is prepared to accept sedation. Despite what her opponents say, she points out that her patients can die with dignity.

KILLING AND LETTING DIE

Pro-euthanasiasts attempt to strengthen their case by arguing that letting a person die (passive euthanasia) is just as bad as taking active steps to end a life (active euthanasia). The result is the same: death. What real difference is there between these two means of achieving it? Doctors sometimes leave patients who are in permanent comas to die. As for those who are struggling with pain, doctors may accelerate their death by drugs, which is allowable when the intention is to relieve pain. Why not administer a direct lethal dosage and end it all quickly? Would this not be more humane?

This raises an interesting question: Is doing nothing the same as doing something? A woman was attacked late at night outside a block of flats in New York. As she screamed and tried to ward off her attacker the lights went on in flat after flat and sleepy residents peered out. Reactions were varied. Some inserted ear plugs and went back to sleep; others wanted to telephone the police but feared being investigated by them; others simply did nothing, later claiming that they always acted on the principle of non-involvement in the affairs of other people. Meanwhile the woman's screams persisted. One man decided eventually to shout out of the window at the attacker; another phoned the police without giving his name. The police, when they arrived, thanked the caller, praised the man who shouted and were disgusted with the others. No legal charge could be brought against them, but morally they were culpable. Yet we would say that though they failed to act, they were not on the same moral par as the attacker of the woman. If they had tried to intervene they could have been badly injured. On the other hand, there was little to prevent them calling the police. The difference between action and nonaction seems to lie in the area of intention. We will look at this shortly.

Doctors act not to harm but to help. Action to terminate a life is irrevocable; there can be no opportunity to re-evaluate it at some later date. But if the patient asks for treatment to be stopped she may reconsider this eventually. As death approaches because the treatment has stopped she may ask for it to be recommenced. 'Letting die' is not irrevocable. On the other hand, if arrangements are made to 'kill' her she may feel that she cannot back out of it, even though she has doubts. Doctors have grave doubts not only about a request to die but about involving themselves in such a killing.[6]

If the patient requests death, this is voluntary euthanasia. But what of non-voluntary euthanasia? The patient is in a vegetative state, and this could hardly be called life as we know it. Drugs are administered to her in order to relieve her of pain, and these have to be increased because the disease becomes increasingly severe. The whole intention is not to terminate life but to relieve pain. There is no question in this country of prolonging suffering or of doctors insisting on operations when there is no benefit to be derived. Particularly difficult are cases of severely mal-formed infants. Decisions to treat or not to treat are taken in conjunction with the family. The criterion which guides these decisions is the capacity of the child to love and be loved so that it is responsive to human care and contact in some sentient way. Even Down's syndrome or spina bifida children can fit into this criterion, though sometimes they are allowed to die. It is judged that this should only happen when 'there is only a biological vestige of life which is pointless and cruel to preserve in its distorted state'.[7]

INTENTION

This appears to be the key issue in deciding whether letting die or killing is wrong. When a doctor takes a patient off a machine he judges that it is pointless to continue the treatment. The patient cannot reach the position of doing without it and therefore she has no hope of recovery. Other patients benefit by such treatment, but since it is obvious that she will not, there is no use in prolonging her pain. She is allowed to die for her own sake; there is no question that the doctor is intending her death. She will die of her basic disease. This procedure is acceptable both morally and legally, for its motive is compassion and there is no deliberate intention to kill. It is a 'letting die'.

James Rachels disagrees, because the result is death. He stresses consequences, not intentions. He argues that intentions tell us something about a person's character, not about their actions. Suppose a military commander is planning an air raid and instructs his air force to bomb an armaments factory. In the event the raid kills some civilians who live nearby. He could have planned that this would happen, or perhaps he did not intend it. But what does it matter, since the result is the same.[8]

This is a strange argument. It opposes moral and legal judgements which are based on motive and intention as well as on the result of an action. Apart from genetic factors, it is motives and intentions that come to predominate in our characters. From these spring attitudes to people and situations. If we had studied over a period of time all the actions of the military commander, we would have been able to judge whether his motives and intentions were caring or callous. We say, 'He is a nice character' or 'She is a wicked person' on the basis of actions. Though we may be mistaken at times, if we have studied the person over a lengthy period we can reach a general opinion. We could then predict whether the military commander was going to plan the operation very carefully so as to avoid hitting the civilians or whether he was the kind of callous person who couldn't care less. It may be that the civilians are very close to the target, and though it is a caring commander who plans carefully to try and avoid them, it happens that deaths ensue. In this case it is not a direct killing but an unfortunate side-effect of a plan aimed at the destruction of the factory.

In hospital, if the doctor intentionally causes harm to the patient by omission, he is just as culpable as if he had committed an error. With regard to 'letting die', the American Medical Association has been careful to insist on the following conditions: the life of the body is being preserved by extraordinary means; there is irrefutable evidence that biological death is imminent; the patient and/or family consents. It is on these conditions and not on any distinction between 'letting die' and killing that the decision is made.

Instead of using these terms, it would be better to speak of permitting a death rather than causing it. A patient who has had every available treatment but shows no signs of recovery and is moving towards death should be permitted to die. To cause her to die would be a direct action and would involve a lethal dosage. This makes the distinction quite clear. In many ways it is the advent of modern technology which has brought these questions to the fore. Earlier, little could be done for handicapped children, many elderly people and patients with damaged brains. But now even if the brain is dead, the breathing and circulation can be maintained artificially. As we have seen, a patient is considered to be dead once the brain has died, so there is no problem in taking such a patient off a machine.

But what about someone whose brain has been severely damaged but has not died? His brain cells do not regenerate and he needs these artificial means. When should treatment stop? It is this kind of question which modern technology has thrust upon us.

WHAT ABOUT THE LAW?

Those who want active euthanasia argue that the law should be changed to permit it, and various proposals have been made as to how this could be done. What is needed is a clear distinction between euthanasia and murder on the basis of motive. Generally mercy killings are dealt with leniently by the courts, but exceptions do arise. A lot of people considered the Roberts case to be a mercy killing, yet the courts ruled for a prison sentence. Others feel that it is necessary always for a manslaughter charge to be brought no matter what the consequences.

But the motive of compassion is irrelevant according to the law as it now stands, for in judgement the stress is put on the deliberate intention to bring about death. Mercy killings, just like murders, involve what the law calls 'malice', and the compassion which motivated the killing is not to the fore in the decision of the courts.

Bills calling for a change have embraced passive, voluntary and non-voluntary euthanasia. Ruth Russell has well expressed the concern which has motivated these Bills: 'What is to be gained by keeping a patient permanently unconscious instead of taking positive steps to induce death if withdrawal of treatment does not cause death?'[9] Included in their proposals have been provision for a person to make an advance declaration of her wishes in the event that she might be suffering from an irremediable condition and, in the case of those who cannot speak for themselves and have not made a prior declaration of their wishes, the agreement of the next of kin or the legal guardian.

What has prevented such Bills, both in the US and England, from being accepted? One reason is that they have been too cumbersome and their safeguards too extensive. James Rachels points out with regard to Bills in America that the patient must first find two witnesses to a petition, which must be filed; then she must obtain a doctor's certificate, see that the petition reaches the court, prove that her disease is terminal, wait while a committee is formed and make sure that it contains two physicians. The committee, having deliberated, will then report back to the court which, if satisfied, will grant the request. The act will then be carried out in the presence of two of the committee's members. Of course, a third party would do most of this, but the patient is likely to be dead before the procedure for bringing about her death gets under way! Rachels is not exaggerating, for Ruth Russell's recommendations for a comprehensive euthanasia Bill have seventeen safeguards. But he wants to go to the other extreme, insisting that it is a simple matter of producing evidence that the patient requested euthanasia and that she was suffering from a terminal illness. With such a difficult and dangerous matter we would need to err in slowness rather than haste.

The changes in English law which have been proposed over the years have stressed the importance of safeguards. The 1969 Bill, which was defeated in the House of Lords by 61 votes to 40, would have empowered doctors to administer euthanasia to adults, but two physicians had to certify that the illness was incurable and caused severe pain. After signature 30 days had to elapse before the act took place. Doctors or nurses who had conscientious objections were excluded from participation.

In 1985 Lord Jenkins of Putney tabled an amendment to

the 1961 Suicide Act which proposed that a person who assisted suicide acted reasonably, in compassion and good faith. This was an oblique way of trying for a modification of the law, relying on the changing attitude towards suicide, but it failed by 48 votes to 15. The composition of the House of Lords represents the elderly strata of the population, and it might have been thought that it was a good place for such a debate. But the vote perhaps reflects a fear of death and of the motives of relatives who might want to bring it about!

It is difficult to enact such a law, due to the variety of the criteria needed to justify it and the complexity of the subject. Writers who have made an exhaustive survey of legal cases in the States declare that the only uncontested area is the competent patient's right to refuse treatment, based on the constitutional right to privacy, which means non-interference. Court judgements have been based on different criteria, such as the best interest of the patient, quality of life and an attempt to analyse what is meant by the term 'competent'. The Supreme Court of the USA has ruled on abortion, and it could do so on euthanasia.

But the debate on euthanasia continued in the UK because of what happened to Nigel Cox and Tony Bland. In 1992 Dr Nigel Cox was convicted of attempted murder for assisting his patient Mrs Lilian Boyes to die. He gave her potassium chloride when she requested to die and her heart stopped. Cox argued that it was a mercy killing and he received a suspended sentence and the condemnation of the General Medical Council. The case of Tony Bland, a young man very badly injured in a football disaster, raised even more controversy. A number of problems arose: How do we distinguish between nursing care and medical treatment; should money be provided to keep him alive when other patients needed it; are food and fluids basic human rights? The doctor contended that he would not recover, for his brain was a mass of liquid and he was unaware of his surroundings. It was medical treatment he was receiving by putting a tube into the stomach to feed him, hence it could be withdrawn.

It is difficult to make a judgement in this complicated case; he could have lived for perhaps another twenty years, but without any quality of life. The situation was intolerable to his parents, and their suffering was taken into account. The intention was to end his life, so it does look like euthanasia in the sense of intentional killing, but the House of Lords committee concluded that the withdrawal of treatment was a letting die. The case also raised the question of what is a person, because his doctor stated that a person is someone who can value life. If this was applied to abortion the foetus could not be valued. When euthanasia was further debated in the light of such events by the Walton committee, it was decided in 1994 that there would be no change in the law because it was impossible to ensure that all acts of euthanasia were voluntary and that a liberalisation of the law could not be abused. The decision was a set-back for the pro-euthanasia lobby who saw it as setting a precedent.

In general, cases of mercy killing both in England and the USA are dealt with more leniently than murder. Ruth Russell has shown that of sixteen cases of direct active euthanasia by non-doctors in the USA between 1832 and 1973, only two resulted in murder convictions; one of the individuals received a life imprisonment and the other, life parole. With regard to eight cases involving doctors only two were convicted on a lesser charge than murder. Judgements regarding passive euthanasia are more complex, especially when it comes to decisions about handicapped children, as Robert Campbell points out. He cites three cases. In the first, a doctor named Arthur allowed a Down's syndrome baby to die and did not carry out a necessary operation to remove an intestinal obstruction. In the second case – that of a child referred to as Baby Doe – it was decided not to offer life-saving treatment. Yet, as Campbell says, in the case known as Re B. an injunction was obtained requiring that the infant – also Down's syndrome – be operated on for the intestinal obstruction.

Although it might not be necessary to go so far as to legalise euthanasia, there would, however, need to be some effort to clear up the disarray in which the law stands, both here and in the USA. But in addition to using the arguments which we have mentioned, anti-euthanasiasts try to strengthen their position by stressing how difficult it is to know when a case is hopeless and what kind of future a deformed child will have. Many handicapped people have inspired us by their achievements, but if the law were changed, such individuals might in future be subjected to a mercy killing when born. Who will protect the minor and the unconscious patient? Do patients really know what they are doing when they are in pain? Can a patient who has made a 'living will' change his mind when he is rushed into hospital? Who administers euthanasia? Ruth Russell proposes the creation of the post of a 'thanatologist' or 'death administrator'! How would patients in hospitals who did not want to die react to his presence? Any Bill proposed in the future will need to be careful both in its proposal and wording. There was a marked deficiency of terminology in the 1969 Bill which ruled that only those who suffered from an incurable illness which caused them severe pain or rendered them incapable of rational existence could be considered legitimate candidates for euthanasia. Opponents of the Bill claimed that this was much too open-ended. Dr Hugh Trowell observed that this definition of legitimacy covered all forms of cancer and leukemia, together with serious coronary disease, many forms of paralysis, cirrhosis (disease of the liver) and numerous other conditions. Since mental diseases deprive a person of his rational powers, most long-term patients in psychiatric hospitals would qualify![10]

It may be that these problems and the other difficulties noted in this section form one of the main reasons why philosophers who consider that euthanasia is morally right do not join in the campaign for its legalisation.

THE CHURCHES

In general, the churches agree that active euthanasia is not permissible. However, they also stress that life should not be prolonged unnecessarily and that it is permissible to administer drugs which relieve pain and may also shorten life. Direct killing, according to a 1981 Report by the Church of Scotland Board of Social Responsibility, would place too big a responsibility on doctors. They would not welcome the task, and it would destroy the trust which now exists between them and their patients. The Report contends for the hospice and believes that the care for the dying which it provides is in accord with the gospel of love for God and one's neighbour.

The Church of England, in its deliberations, does take note of the special emergencies which can arise in accidents, war and remote places. In such situations, in the absence of pain-killing drugs, it could be necessary to kill. A soldier wounded in the jungle begs his companion to kill him because he knows that if he falls into the hands of the enemy they will torture him for information. A lorry driver is trapped in a burning vehicle; it is better that he dies quickly rather than slowly in the flames. These are exceptional cases, and we will refer to them later. But we cannot base a change of the law on such emergencies and on conditions different to those which operate in our hospitals.

The Church of England argues that before the law on euthanasia could be changed, evidence would need to be presented to show that an alteration would remove greater evils than it would cause. The danger might be that euthanasia could become widespread and be performed for unsound reasons.

The Catholic Church has the doctrine of double effect. Death is the side-effect of an action intended to relieve pain. The relief of pain, which is absolutely necessary, outweighs the possibility that death may eventually ensue as drug administration increases. But the doctrine is not acceptable to all. Some contend that it is slow euthanasia for drugs are being used that will kill, it is hypocritical and dishonest and an easy way out of the situation, and a fudging of the facts. Defenders of the doctrine answer that they are using diamorphine or morphine starting with a small dose and increasing it to relieve the pain. They point out that it is difficult to kill a patient with these drugs hence when direct killing was intended Dr Nigel Cox had to turn to potassium chloride which stopped the heart of his patient. But how are we to measure the evil effect of death against the relief of pain? In terminal cases it is all right, for the patient is going to die and the doctor's duty is to relieve pain and make her as comfortable as possible.

The Catholic Church distinguishes between ordinary and extraordinary treatment. Ordinary treatment is medicines, techniques and operations which offer a reasonable hope of benefit and can be obtained and used without excessive pain and other inconvenience. Extraordinary treatment is expensive, involves pain and may not offer a reasonable hope of benefit, but may also prove to be very effective and may advance research. A doctor may decide to rule out extraordinary measures if they involve pain and will not benefit the patient. But patients have insisted on these, claiming them as their right. Again, there is set up a tension between the autonomy of the patient and what the doctor judges to be best. If the measure would save the patient's life, no treatment is too expensive. But if the patient's life is coming to an end anyway, or if she is not terminal but cannot expect any reasonable quality of life, then the decision may be not to use such measures.[11]

Another difficulty is that the terms 'ordinary' and 'extra-ordinary' are very flexible, so that what may be ordinary for one patient is extraordinary for another. James Rachels thinks that we should set aside all this terminology and simply ask the question: What is best for the patient? He thinks active termination can be the best solution in many cases.

But since Christianity in general holds strongly to this principle of the sanctity of life, any taking of life, even in the context of suffering, requires strong justification. In general Christianity opposes euthanasia not only in the UK but in the Greek and Russian Orthodox Churches, the Episcopal Church in America and the Evangelical Lutheran Church. But in the Presbyterian Church of America during 1983 it was stated that if the illness is terminal voluntary euthanasia is allowed and this agrees with the United Methodists who in 1986 accepted the doctrine of double effect. Christianity also agrees with those philosophers who contend that 'doing nothing' is at times as bad as 'doing something'. Jesus stood in the prophetic tradition of 'doing justly and loving mercy', and his story of the Good Samaritan emphasises that love of one's neighbour is doing something for the wounded man. In another of Jesus' stories a rich man is condemned because he never noticed or attended to a poor beggar at his gate (Luke 16:19).

Christianity is positive, as we see in the Golden Rule: 'Do unto others as you would have them do unto you' (Matthew 7:12). James Rachels and R. M. Hare interpret this as meaning, when applied to euthanasia, that it cannot be absolutely wrong. Rachels poses the question: Suppose you were told that you would either die quietly and without pain at the age of eighty, or else a few days later, having suffered severe pain during that short extra lease of life? What would you choose? We would not want a rule applied to us which excluded the first option, so why should we want to apply it to others?

Hare has a vivid example. The driver of a petrol lorry is involved in an accident in which his tanker is overturned and immediately catches fire. He is trapped in the cab and cannot be freed. He beseeches the bystanders to kill him by hitting him on the head so that he will not roast to death. Such an incident did in fact happen. Somebody did as the driver asked, but Hare cannot remember what happened in the courts afterwards. He puts the question: What would you want people to do to you if you were in the situation of the driver?

Taking these examples as the basis of their argument, the philosophers allege that both Christianity and Immanuel Kant ironically appear to be disobeying the Golden Rule. Kant's categorical imperative was a philosophical version of the Christian Golden Rule, and he opposed mercy killing as contrary not to revelation but reason.

But it is not apparent that either Christianity or medical practice would prevent a bringing to an end of a terminal agony. The BMA Report cites a possible incident not unlike Hare's. A person is trapped by twisted steelwork in the onrushing path of a fire in a burning hotel. The firemen say they cannot effect a rescue, and it is clear that the fire will inevitably burn the person to death. He pleads to be killed, as the wounds caused by the steelwork are agonisingly painful. Also he is in anguish at the thought of the dreadful way in which he is going to die. What should the doctor do? The Report says, 'We believe that the doctor should ensure that the patient does not suffer. An appropriate dose of medication should be given to ensure that the patient is not conscious of his terminal agony.'[12]

Christianity would agree. Life is not to be preserved at all costs, for death is not to be feared. It is a transition, not a terminus. Compassion and love can override commandments, as shown by the ministry of Jesus. But what is emphasised is that emergencies and exceptional cases should not be allowed to become the basis for a theory which would seek to make rules against killing redundant.

EUTHANASIA IN EUROPE AND ELSEWHERE

A brief discussion of practice elsewhere will widen the context of our understanding of euthanasia. In France, Denmark, Sweden and the Federal Republic of Germany people are generally opposed to euthanasia, as they are in England. But incurable patients are sometimes helped to die in these countries, and such cases are brought before the courts. Dr Leon Schwartzenberg, the best-known cancer specialist in France, was suspended for a year by his regional medical council. He does not believe that there is any difference between relieving pain and ending life. He has received support for this view from the French Minister of Health, and the media have called for the abolition of the medical councils.

In the Netherlands a doctor is permitted to terminate life if the patient requests it and he follows these legal guidelines:

(i) The patient has to be informed about his situation.

(ii) The physician must have become convinced that the patient's request to terminate his life is the result of careful consideration and that he has upheld his request freely.

(iii) The physician must have come to the judgement that termination of the life of the patient is justified, because the only alternative is the present untenable situation.

(iv) The physician must have consulted one of the physicians named in a list drawn up by the Minister of Health.

The BMA Report, unlike some other reports on the Dutch scene, says that such guidelines have helped doctors who had previously been carrying through euthanasia 'surreptitiously' for fear of prosecution. However, the Report also notes the opposition from certain bodies of opinion, usually on religious grounds, to this active termination of life. They fear it will replace good terminal care, undermine the trust that the patient has in the doctor, encourage relatives to pressurise patients to request death and lead to the slippery slope of involuntary euthanasia. It is reckoned that there are over 5,000 deaths per year in the Netherlands due to actions aimed at terminating a person's life at his explicit request. Opponents of the practice put the figure at a much higher level and contend that it has led to abuse and fear on the part of the elderly.[13]

In contrast to the practice in the Netherlands, America tends to do everything possible to prolong life, even when there is a hopeless prognosis. Patients are placed on respirators or have major surgery, and in general this practice deserves the criticisms which Rachels and others make of it. Once a treatment is started there is great reluctance to discontinue it, since such action may lead to a court case.

The BMA Report says, 'Many States have now endeavoured to provide further guidance for difficult ethical decisions by allowing patients to make advance declarations of what treatments they are prepared to accept.'[14]

Dr Jack Kervorkian has been the centre of much attention in America and is known as 'Dr Death'. It was estimated that by 1996 he had killed forty patients, but prosecutions against him failed until 1999 when he was sent to prison for administering a lethal injection to a patient on TV! He defended himself in court and wanted a debate on euthanasia, but the judge ruled it out. He provided a device with which the patient, by pushing a button, could kill herself. In Australia the Northern Territory voted euthanasia into law on 25 May 1995, but the federal parliament revoked the law in March 1997. The influence of Dr Philip Nitschke on such legislation was apparent. He invented a computer programme which enabled the terminally ill to take their own lives by pressing a button which administered lethal drugs. It was used by cancer victim Bob Dent.

CONCLUSION

In most of the problems that we are considering the right of the individual does conflict with the laws and paternalism of society. From the medical viewpoint, euthanasia could involve the profession in a harmful situation. Doctors and nurses seek to preserve life, and it would create a crisis if patients thought that they were 'ready to kill where they cannot cure'.[15] What kind of society would we have if patients were pressurised to think that they were a nuisance to all concerned? Suicide does not involve another person, either friend or doctor, but euthanasia does and therefore is more complex. James Rachels thinks that when a patient requests a lethal drug and the doctor provides it, this is a 'private affair'. Those participating are 'consenting adults' and no one else's interests need be involved. But can the relation of doctor and patient be a private affair? Has he not got duties and a responsibility which put him in a position different to that of a 'consenting adult'? This term applies to sexual relations, not medical care. The doctor must answer to his colleagues, his hospital administration and the law for what he does. He is not conducting a private affair with a patient!

The medical viewpoint and religious one concur that in emergencies active euthanasia may be necessary to relieve a terminal agony. Here the intention is to alleviate suffering, not to kill. The question of intention is very important, as we have seen. They also agree that there is no point in prolonging life, as Pope Pius XII confirmed in 1957. He asserted that when nothing was left but the 'simple life of organs' it was not wise to seek to prolong life. He also said that 'If the actual administration of drugs brings about two distinct effects, the one the relief of pain, the other the shortening of life, the action is lawful.'[16]

Humanism places the stress on the individual's right to die but also on the avoidance of hurt to others. It concurs with the medical and religious viewpoints on the dignity of human life and the prevention of cruelty, but would permit an intervention by another person to terminate suffering.

The difference between the Humanist and the Christian often lies in the debate about who controls our lives. Christianity argues that life is the gift of God, but the Humanist contends for a person's self-control over their own destiny. Yet both Christian and Humanist are wary about the possible abuse of euthanasia. Michael Ignatieff, writing from a Humanist point of view, says that he would support a right to choose to die if he was sure that it would not be abused: 'Most societies outlaw euthanasia not because they are convinced that it is wrong in every instance, but because they know there is no other way to keep it under control. It is because the line between euthanasia and failing to care is so fine that society has to draw a gross legal furrow.'[17] But in exceptional cases of intolerable suffering where as a last resort mercy killing takes place (e.g. the Roberts and Johnson cases which we noted at the beginning of the chapter), it would be helpful if there was some change in the law which allowed the charge of manslaughter to be made rather than that of murder. In such cases those who help the sufferers to die do so for purely compassionate reasons.

Humanists may gain some encouragement by the debate that is currently going on among Christian thinkers on voluntary euthanasia. Some do advocate it on the basis of the Dutch legal system. They deny that this would lead to involuntary euthanasia or cause public alarm particularly among the elderly. Death is not the ultimate evil and Christians should welcome it following the example of the apostle Paul (1 Timothy 4:6–8). A swift death of one's own choosing (Scripture does not condemn suicide) is better than a lingering life of sickness.[18] It is interesting that these Christian thinkers believe in God and an after-life, unlike Humanists, yet agree with them regarding voluntary euthanasia. Others, however, argue that this position does not recognise the sanctity of life as laid down in the Bible, or take into account the scriptural context of war where suicides occur, or that the taking of life is a violation of the divine image in us, or pays attention to the doctrine of double effect. It places too much stress on personal consent, ignores the relational context in which we live and relies on the utilitarian principle of minimising suffering.[19]

In reply it is contended that the majority in Britain (82 per cent in 1996) now want voluntary euthanasia, the sanctity of life is not an absolute value, and just as almost all Christian leadership apart from the Vatican has come to terms with birth control so 'sooner or later will Chistian leadership have to come to terms with death control'.[20] The debate continues!

Euthanasia is the claim to control the timing of one's own death. In the next chapter we face an even sharper issue and ask the question: Has a woman the right to ask for an abortion when she wants it and cause the death of the unborn?

Questions for discussion
- If we could devise appropriate safeguards to ensure that the decision to opt for euthanasia was both informed and voluntary would there be any further arguments against permitting voluntary euthanasia?
- Can active euthanasia ever be morally justified?
- Can we really distinguish between killing and letting die?
- Since suicide is legal why can we not assist people to die?

THREE

Killing the Unborn

Having an abortion appears to be easier today since a surgical process has been replaced by a natural one. It is a pill known as RU486 or mifepristone, which originated in France and when taken blocks the receptors in the lining of the womb. The result is that the womb walls break down and there is a spontaneous abortion. The pill has been marketed in France, Britain and other countries, but there are side-effects of pain and heavy bleeding and it is difficult to estimate the long-term effects. A woman can get the pill from licensed clinics as soon as she knows she is pregnant, and need not be detained in hospital. Hence it does away with the long waiting lists in abortion clinics.

Of course, today the reasons for abortion are many. Among them are saving the mother's life and protecting her health. Sometimes the reasons are social or economic. Many contend that abortion should be freely available on demand, and that women should have the right to choose it when they are confronted with an unwanted pregnancy. Those who oppose abortion on demand ask:

— Will disposable foetuses lead to disposable people?
— Can a woman in an emotionally disturbed frame of mind due to a pregnancy really decide properly?

— Will there not be regrets later?
— Could there be an effect on future child-bearing?

Two organisations in this country confront one another over this issue – the Abortion Law Reform Association (ALRA) and the Society for the Protection of the Unborn Child (SPUC). The former, founded in 1936, has moved towards the demand for abortion to be freely granted on the request of the mother. The latter, founded much later, strongly campaigns for special safeguards and care for children, and insists that human life should only be taken in cases of urgent necessity. They consider the 1967 Abortion Act, which we will see has been amended, as too liberal and argue that it paved the way for the present rising tide of abortions in this country.

WHAT DOES THE ACT REALLY SAY?

It says that abortion is acceptable if two doctors agree that continuing the pregnancy involves a greater risk to the mother's life, or to her mental or physical health, or to the mental or physical health of the existing children in the family than abortion does. Abortion is also permissible in cases where there is a substantial risk that the child will be born seriously deformed. Since a wide interpretation can be placed on the term 'her mental and physical health' and doctors and psychiatrists can differ, the door to abortion tends to be open on request. Taking the health of the existing children in the family as a factor to be considered makes the door even more likely to open. The mother may be mentally distressed about the effect on her family of having another child, especially if their budget is already under strain and their housing is inadequate. This so-called 'social clause' is based on utilitarian considerations of the greatest happiness of the greatest number. When mother, father and family all agree that another child would upset their happiness, the logical step is abortion. Of course, the Act never intended this, but many allege it is so loosely worded and can be interpreted in so many different ways that this is the net result.

According to Rex Gardner, a gynaecologist, abortion demand is not only steadily increasing but the pressure on doctors, nurses and hospitals in general is so enormous that it is becoming more difficult to refuse abortion on request. Not only did the Act underestimate the flood of applications for the operation, but it was applied 'in the breach rather than in the observance'. Gardner writes:

> The doctors' surgeries, the hospital out-patient departments, the private clinics, are today thronged with a host of women seeking to get rid of their pregnancies. Some have been brainwashed into equating 'the unwanted pregnancy' with 'unwanted child' and make a journey they will one day regret. Some are careless members of the permissive society with no sense of responsibility either for their behaviour or for their coming child. Some are worn-out women burdened by long years of child-bearing and child-rearing who seek well deserved relief. The majority do not fall neatly into any of these categories.[1]

I suppose one answer to this which would be given by the ALRA is that at least they are at licensed clinics and not hazarding their lives at back-street places.

The philosopher and the religious thinker are concerned with the law and its workings. Philosophers consider whether it is right for the law to concern itself with matters where there is so much disagreement, and they also ask how it is possible to legislate for the unborn. But most thinking centres on the moral issues involved:

— Has the foetus in the womb any moral status, and what are the claims of the mother in opposition to it?
— Is the foetus a person or a potential person?
— Can we kill innocent human beings (assuming that the foetus is to be considered a human being at its various stages of development)?

It is these questions and others concerned with morality that we intend concentrating on in this chapter.

THE DIFFERENT VIEWS

There are positions to the right and the left. The conservatives contend that the foetus is a human being from conception. Sometimes this belief has been based on the religious concept of a soul which enters then, but today it is usually based on the idea that there is no moral difference between this moment and other stages of development that could be chosen. Against those who say that abortion is illegitimate only when the foetus can survive independent of the mother, the conservative replies that medical science may soon push this back to conception itself. In any case, it seems ridiculous to make the foetus' viability depend on the state of medical science in a particular country, so that we might say: 'It is able to be independent of the mother in America but not in Africa,' or 'It's not possible today, but perhaps next year, as medical science advances.'

Left of the conservative is the extreme liberal who regards the foetus as just another piece of tissue. He is not worried about abortion at any stage. The mother can do what she likes with her body, so what is all the fuss about? Some liberals think that the foetus is on a level with animals and that those who have no conscience about killing animals should not hesitate in the case of a foetus. The conservative will not allow the liberal to get away with these arguments. He points out that a woman has not the right to harm her body; indeed, we have laws against anything – drugs, for example – that might cause such injury. Further, the foetus is not like an animal or piece of tissue; it is a special part of the woman, a growing, living organism with which she is going to form a loving relation. And even if we agree that the foetus is on a level with animals, there is still a problem, since there are many people who consider that killing animals is not only offensive but morally wrong.

Many people, however, feel that the solution to most problems is compromise, and so we have a middle-of-the-road view which is called the 'mixed strategy'. It tells us to look at what is going on in the womb of the mother as the organism moves from zygote to embryo to foetus to baby. What we see is a sliding scale of development, so that in the early stages there is no thinking, feeling, moving around or the doing of the things that we associate with human beings. But in the later stages these are all there. So a late abortion must only be undertaken for a very serious reason, such as saving the mother's life. But in the early stages abortion can be granted for most of the reasons specified by the 1967 Act. Neither conservative nor liberal finds this view completely satisfactory, and it must be said that it is somewhat hazy about the moral status of the foetus in the middle stages of development.

A final view, which many people think is attractive, is what is called 'potentiality'. The foetus is regarded as morally unique from its conception. It cannot be compared with other parts of the body and is unlike an animal in being distinctly human. Only in the early stages is abortion permissible. There must be a good reason for it, such as the possibility or certainty of the baby being born with abnormalities.

Whatever may be said for or against these various views, it is apparent that the way in which we think of this organism in the womb and the characteristics we might consider it to have will be determining factors in our seeking to morally justify an abortion.

LIFE IN THE WOMB

Pictures of what is going on in the womb of the mother have changed the opinion of people regarding abortion. The ovum of the woman is fertilised by the male and becomes a single-cell zygote with twenty-three pairs of chromosomes, one in each pair coming from each parent. By the third day after conception it has divided into a multicell zygote which moves through the Fallopian tube into the uterus over a period of four to five days and then implants in the uterine wall. This implantation takes six to eight days and is complete eleven to thirteen days after fertilisation. It is estimated that at least 40 per cent of all zygotes fail to implant successfully, and of those that do a further 20 per cent are lost due to miscarriage.

About this time the zygote is renamed an embryo. At implantation its first feature appears. For this reason the Warnock Report set the fourteenth day after fertilisation as the cut-off point for permissible research. It is startling to realise, considering the fact that abortion is now permitted up to twenty-four weeks in this country, that as early as the seventeenth day characteristics such as nerve cells, blood cells and skin cells begin. Within three weeks rudimentary eyes, ears and kidneys develop, as well as the beginnings of the liver, the stomach and the nervous system. The blood system begins to function independently at this time and the head is visible. Eight weeks after fertilisation the embryo, now known as the foetus, has arms, legs, fingers and toes, makes squirming and kicking movements and has even been observed sucking its thumb!

What happens in the argument between the conservative and liberal is that the former places weight on the foetus' similarities with the human person whereas the latter stresses the dissimilarities, and thus the impasse. Both positions have their difficulties. Morality has to do with persons, and the conservative, when he calls a tiny cluster of cells a person, has a hard task convincing many people. The liberal, on the other hand, will abort just before birth but will not kill babies after birth and wants us to believe that location or geography determines the foetus' moral status. Those who hold the potential view have the job of demonstrating that having the potential to become a person is of the same value as actually being a person. Is an acorn of the same value as a tree? Is a foetus as valuable as a child which has actually been born? All other views must show that their boundary line for abortion, whether it is at implantation or at the time of the foetus being able to survive independent of the mother, is morally correct. Certainly, this question of independence has its own problems, for if the baby were to be delivered in the twentieth week it could possibly survive in an incubator, and would have an almost sure chance if delivered in the twenty-fifth week. But it is not independent and needs much care and help – with its breathing, for example. Without such care it will not survive. As we have seen, this ability to survive will be pushed further back as medical science advances.

IS THE FOETUS A PERSON?

It comes as a surprise to most of us that philosophers distinguish between a human being and a person. A human being belongs to a certain class of beings and has characteristics which makes him different from the animals. Scientifically he is the highest point of the evolutionary scale. We show our respect for him by the rule, 'You shall not kill human beings.' But could we not be accused of favouring a certain class of beings with this rule? What about other animals, such as the cow, which is sacred to the Hindus? Indeed, to the Buddhist every living creature is sacred. As Albert Schweitzer pointed out, it is necessary to have a reverence for all of life. But recent philosophical writing does not seem to have retained that respect.

Michael Tooley points out that a machine is not capable of being conscious of what it is or of having desires. It is only in science fiction movies that the computer suddenly astounds its creator by desiring to do things for which it has not been programmed. We recognise that a machine's inability to desire to do other than what it has been programmed to do means that it does not have rights. But a person has desires and realises that he has a self and experience of a continuing nature. The foetus, says Tooley, is more like a machine, since it does not have such desires or concepts. Tooley then bases rights on desires and being conscious of having a self.

But what, then, of a person who is unconscious or brainwashed and thus has no desires or the wrong ones? Are their rights lost? Tooley replies that she must retain her rights, particularly the right to life, because she would desire this if she were not under these conditions. The ability to have the desire to live is still there, and this is the deciding factor.

However, the list of exceptions can be extended. We can mention senile persons, who still have rights even though they have no relevant desires. And there are infants, who have the right to property even though they do not have either the concept or the desire. Is it really necessary for us to understand something before we can desire it? A baby has desires, especially for its mother's milk, without any understanding of what it is doing. When is this infant going to measure up to Tooley's sophisticated idea of what a person is? Does his position not imply infanticide as well as abortion? Tooley appears to draw back here, not wanting to grant infanticide, even though his definition calls for it. Instead he says that it is permissible only in the case of babies born with severe defects. Tooley also appears to be inconsistent about what he calls non-persons – that is, animals. For example, according to him a cat has the right not to be tortured but as a non-person can be killed. But if it has the right not to be tortured should it not also have the right not to be killed?

Tooley rejects the potentiality argument with regard to the foetus. Imagine a young child who has the right to an estate but has not the conceptuality of wanting the estate. We might think that such a potential right would guarantee him the estate at a future time and give him a certain status with regard to it, but Tooley argues: 'My inclination is to say that the correct description is not that the child now has a right to the estate but that he will come to have such a right when he is mature . . . he cannot do things with the estate such as selling it or giving it away that he will be able to do later on.'[2]

Peter Singer, another philosopher, chooses a very prominent person for his illustration. Prince Charles is potentially King of England, but Singer says that does not give him the rights of a king. But against this we can argue that as heir apparent he has certain rights which we do not have. These will include special education, protection, guidance, a salary and so on. The heir to an estate or kingship eventually inherits what has always been his right from birth. In English and American law cases the unborn child has been adjudged to own property and possess rights.[3]

This is known as the retrospective procedure, and it is something which the law accepts. There is the Congenital Disabilities (Civil Liability) Act 1976, which allows, in limited circumstances, damages to be recovered by a person who was in his or her mother's womb injured through the negligence of some third person? The embryo or foetus is thus accorded a kind of retrospective status. This would appear to support the potentiality argument, at least in the legal sense.

According to Tooley's definition the infant is less a person than the adult. But if a fireman had to decide whether to save an adult or a child from a burning building, it is not obvious that he would choose to save the adult. In fact, since the infant will normally have the greater lifespan, he may concentrate his efforts on saving it, and if there is a mother and child she may insist that he saves her child. Both the fireman and the mother, it would seem, place a tremendous value on the life of the child, recognising it as a 'small person'.

Other philosophers, realising the difficulty of defining the word 'person' say that we should concentrate on the term 'human being', despite the charge of favouring such a class of being which we have noted. It is sufficient, they think, to say that the baby was born of human parents, or else they argue that the terms 'person' and 'human being' are roughly interchangeable and not different concepts, as Tooley says. Suppose, then, we decide to accept that the foetus is a human being or person from the time of conception. Is there then a possibility of still contending for abortion? This is certainly worth considering.

RIVAL CLAIMS TO LIFE

Suppose you wake up one morning and find yourself in bed with a famous violinist! When you recover from the shock you discover that you have been kidnapped and that your bloodstream has been hooked up to him, for it happens that he has an ailment which will kill him unless you share your kidneys for a period of nine months. He will be unconscious all that time and you will have to stay in bed. Only after nine months will he be unplugged. It is essential that you agree to this, since only you have the right type of blood. Without your co-operation he will die.

Judith Thomson thinks that this is a good analogy to the condition of a woman carrying a child. But it has its obvious flaws. A pregnant woman does not have to stay in bed for nine months and her relation with what is in her womb is much more personal and intimate. Indeed, pregnancy is unique and no perfect analogy can be found. The Thomson analogy is more appropriate to a rape case since the woman has been forced into the situation with the violinist.[4]

Thomson is willing to assume that the foetus is a person from conception and says that some people then go on to argue that in a rape case the foetus is innocent and must not be killed. Others think that even in a case where the mother will die if the foetus is not aborted she has no right to save her life. Thomson challenges both arguments, saying that the mother's life must be saved when the foetus is threatening her and that abortion is permissible in the case of rape. A woman can rightly say, 'This is *my* body,' and decide freely what happens to it. Just as she has the right to unplug the violinist, she has the right to request abortion. But the woman in the violinist analogy has been forced into a situation, and therefore, as we noted, the analogy would appear to apply only to rape cases and not to cases where the intercourse has been voluntary. With regard to the mother's life being at stake, the analogy does not fit, since the violinist is not threatening his bedmate's life as the foetus is threatening the mother's life. But Thomson is correct to argue that the violinist has no right to the use of the woman's kidneys. Permission to use them must be freely given and is really an act of compassion, just like the blood donor's giving of his blood. People do, of course, offer the use of their organs, and think that in some way it is morally right that they should. Charity does play a role in our relations with others.

Suppose, however, that the woman has entered voluntarily into the arrangement with the violinist, just as a woman by voluntary intercourse becomes pregnant. Is there not a responsibility here? To cope with this question, Thomson uses another analogy. A woman opens a window because it is hot in her bedroom, and a burglar climbs in. Is she responsible for his intrusion? The woman voluntarily opened the window, but she did not want the burglar to enter, so she cannot be responsible for it. Thomson then argues that a woman is not responsible when voluntary intercourse results in a pregnancy. It is clear that the analogy does not fit. A pregnancy (it is understood that contraception has failed) is the result of a voluntary act on the part of two people. The act is enjoyable and welcome, but the pregnancy isn't. While the woman is not responsible for the burglar being there, the couple are responsible for the pregnancy. The burglar is not like the foetus; he is there by deliberate intent, but the foetus is not. Thomson appears to see that her argument is weak on this question of pregnancies due to normal intercourse, and she says that if it is indeed weak it would be better to leave the matter open. Hence we can conclude that here we have many and not 'some' cases where abortion seems impermissible.

To be fair, however, Thomson is concerned with mercy and compassion as well as justice. This is necessary, for morality relates not only to justice between persons but also to acts of charity. We often condemn people who, like Shylock, demand their pound of flesh and forget the quality of mercy. Hence Thomson turns to the story of the Good Samaritan (Luke 10:30–35). In going out of his way to help the wounded man he displayed the quality of charity. She gives a new twist to the interpretation by saying that both the priest and the Levite were not even Minimally Decent Samaritans, for they did nothing for the man. After telling the story Jesus told his hearers to go and do likewise, and Thomson admits that he may have been calling on people to do more than is morally required of them. But she thinks that we are not required to act like Good Samaritans, for such behaviour may mean the risk of death. She takes this view despite the command of Jesus to act as the Good Samaritan did. What she says is that we should act as Minimally Decent Samaritans, which could mean telling someone at the next village that the wounded man needed help. I am not compelled to stop and help someone who is lying by the roadside, having been beaten up by thieves, for there is always the risk that they may still be around! Thus Thomson sets aside not only what this story teaches but also one of the essential themes of the New Testament. That is, that acting in a Christian way involves risk and danger. The fact that the law does not even compel me to ring the police when I see someone being beaten up or murdered does not mean that my inaction should not be morally condemned. Thomson indeed admits that there is a gross injustice in the existing state of the law, for it does not even compel me to be a Minimally Decent Samaritan.

The way of the Good Samaritan would demand a large sacrifice, and some people would call it and the whole Christian ethic idealistic. But we will leave this matter until later, when we will be discussing the Christian law of love. Minimally Decent Samaritans would not, according to Thomson, agree to the violinist being in the bed for such a long period of time. Hence abortion for rape is permissible. Women who had an unwanted pregnancy due to the failure of contraception would also be permitted to have an abortion. But, as Thomson admits, the Good Samaritan would not act in this way, even if the social and economic conditions were difficult. Of course, a Minimally Decent Samaritan would not request an abortion merely because she wanted a holiday abroad or she wished to continue with her career. But real sacrifice is not required of her.

Thomson, however, while not asking for great sacrifices is admitting that actions can be wrong not only when they are unjust but also when they are cruel, callous and selfish. Hence she condemns the Levite and the priest in the parable. But let us look at what she makes paramount, namely the rights of the woman over her body. In his book, *Causing Death and Saving Lives* (1977), Jonathan Glover finds fault here, arguing that you do not refer to your body in the same way as you think of your house or coat and that property rights do not have the moral weight that Thomson is giving to them. If you are standing beside a river and see two drowning people reaching for the same lifebelt you do not intervene to make sure that it is the owner who gets it! Should the doctor make his decision to carry out an abortion simply on the grounds that the foetus is occupying property belonging to the mother? We think not. The foetus needs the woman's body to survive. While

Thomson argues that it is not unjust for her to refuse, she admits that abortion is an uncharitable act.

Again, if the pregnancy has resulted from normal intercourse it could be argued that the woman has given the foetus the right to be there. In the case of rape, this is not so; hence most of what Thomson says is applying to that particular situation. But Thomson will not admit this, as we have seen. In fact she moves towards a liberal abortion policy under which a woman who initially wanted a baby could change her mind in the course of the pregnancy and ask for an abortion.

There is also a problem about the rape case, given the fact that Thomson is assuming that the foetus is a person. Are we not at times called to be responsible for something or somebody for which or whom we have not voluntarily assumed responsibility? We all follow a routine of duties and are responsible for persons in various ways, and then suddenly something is thrust upon us, like the Good Samaritan finding a man by the roadside. He assumes responsibility for him, but in strict justice he does not need to, as Thomson would say. However, to be callous and pass by would be as bad as being unjust, according to her. So it would seem that she is saying that one would have to think carefully before requesting an abortion, even though not having an abortion would entail great sacrifice.

If, then, the conservative view that the foetus is a person is used as a basis for such an argument, the conclusion might be a restriction rather than a liberalising of abortion. However, as we have seen, the liberal does not accept that the foetus is a person, so in his view abortion on demand is permissible. Those who hold the more moderate view tend to grant abortion only when the mother's life is at stake, or when without it there may be physical or psychological harm to the mother, or for the benefit of the infant, who may be born with severe defects, or in the case of rape.

WHAT ABOUT THE HANDICAPPED?

In a recent radio programme a man who had been blind for 25 years said that he wished he had never been born. Asked if he had ever considered suicide, he said that he had thought about it but was too much of a coward to do it. On the other hand, some of those who phoned in spoke of the joy that a handicapped child had brought into their family, and others were glad that their parents did not agree to an abortion because they were born only slightly handicapped. This difficulty of detecting disability is one of the reasons why parents do hesitate regarding an abortion. In the particular case of foetuses with spina bifida, the medical profession is divided, some doctors arguing for termination, others pointing out that many who have been born have developed useful and worthwhile lives. An indication of the difficulty of making such decisions is the number of cases where the courts have overruled both the wishes of parents and the decisions of doctors. But the screening of pregnant women does take place, and if spina bifida is detected the mother will be offered an abortion. The same applies to those foetuses affected by Down's syndrome.

Certainly, it is by no means certain that abortion should be carried out simply because a child is likely to be handicapped, as this remarkable statement by Mrs Alison Davis shows: 'I was born with severe spina bifida and am confined to a wheelchair as a result. Despite my disability and the gloomy predictions made by doctors at my birth, I am now leading a very full, happy and satisfying life by any standards.' And again, responding to a proposal for a reform of the law concerning disabled newborn infants, she has this to say:

> I am 28 years old, and suffer from a severe physical disability which is irreversible, as defined by the Bill . . . [the Bill] suggests several criteria for predicting the potential quality of life of people like me, and I note that I should have 'no worthwhile quality of life'. Despite my disability I went to an ordinary school and then to university, where I gained an honours degree in sociology. I now work full-time defending the right to life of handicapped people. I have been married eight years to an able bodied man, and over the years we have travelled widely in Europe, the Soviet Union and the United States. This year we plan to visit the Far East. Who would say I have 'no worthwhile quality of life'?[5]

PRINCIPLES?

Abortion raises in an acute form the question of the taking of an innocent human life. Hence those who hold the principle that it is always wrong to kill the innocent rule abortion out. But, as we saw in the last chapter, emergencies can occur both in war and in everyday accidents in which it is a compassionate act to kill, and this applied to the euthanasia cases which we discussed. What we noted was that intentional killing, where a person wanted to be rid of someone or deliberately planned an action so that innocent people might be killed, was wrong. Now we have seen that some defend abortion against such a principle by saying that the foetus is not yet a human being or a person.

We have noted that this is debatable and difficult to justify. But those who follow a utilitarian line of reasoning stress the consequences of actions and often approve an abortion if it results in happiness for the mother and all concerned. The principle of the greatest happiness of the greatest number will operate with a watchful eye not only on the happiness of the family unit but also on that of society as a whole. A liberal and permissive abortion policy would be right in an overpopulated society but not in an underpopulated one.

Killing a foetus may be right in some circumstances but wrong in others. It all depends on what course of action will maximise happiness and has little to do with the principle of the sanctity of life or the idea that life is intrinsically valuable. The utilitarian approach can also conflict with a person's right to life, since it may be better that he dies so that the happiness of the many may be increased. Basically utilitarianism separates agent and action, so that even though a person may be callous and hard-hearted, if his action produces happiness, it is all right. But as we have noted in previous chapters, we cannot separate motive, intention and action in judging what a person has done.

The existentialist position has difficulties too. It contends that abortion is a choice made by the mother. She cannot base this on what she has learned from any moral code, but has the freedom to agonise over what is the right thing to do in her particular circumstances. But there are many people involved in an abortion: doctors, nurses, the father, relatives, counsellors and probably social workers. Advice is likely to be at hand and welcome and, despite what the existentialist says, this will in all likelihood sway the mother in her decision. Social factors such as the health of the child to be born and the effect of the addition of another member to what may already be a large family, will play a role in the making of a decision. The utilitarian would argue that a child who will be born handicapped will not have a 'worthwhile life'. But how are we to decide this? The case of Alison Davis makes us think about it very carefully. Medical technology is now able to foretell the sort of diseases from which an individual will suffer, so the mother can be advised whether to have an abortion or not. As such technology advances it may be possible to predict whether foetuses are liable to suffer congenital defects at some point in their lives, and this raises all kinds of questions. Should a foetus be aborted when it is foreseen that blindness or deafness will occur at some point and make the individual miserable? If this technology had been available in the past, what advice would have been given to the mothers of Milton and Beethoven? Just as medical technology poses problems about keeping patients alive and raises the question of euthanasia, it also affects decisions regarding abortion. While it can offer help to those born suffering from inherited diseases, it needs to be carefully watched and controlled, particularly when decisions have to be made about a 'worthwhile life'.

Basically utilitarianism proceeds on the basis of the side-effects on others in the case of abortion. But if euthanasia is carried out for the sake of the person concerned and not for the benefit of relatives, then it can be argued that more weight should be given to the best interests of the foetus. Abortion is then right if it is really proposed for the sake of the unborn child. Often it is the health of the mother that receives the first consideration. This seems appropriate when to have the child might cause her death. But if it is a case of a lesser physical risk or of danger to her mental health, there are greater difficulties, for life is of greater value than health. Here it is a question of weighing the life of the foetus against the health of the mother.

THE CHRISTIAN TEACHING

Imagine being granted an abortion on the grounds that pregnancy has an ugly effect on a woman's figure! Yet in Roman and Greek society, which thought nothing of infanticide, this was the kind of trivial reason that enabled a woman to get an abortion. No doubt money and power made it easier, as always happens. Ancient society's attitude to women and children stands in contrast to that of early Christianity. Women and children had a special place in the ministry of Jesus, and the early Church pleaded for the innocent life to be preserved and condemned abortion. One of the earliest statements is in the Didache: 'You shall not kill the child in womb or murder a new born infant.' This attitude was maintained during the first three centuries by Tertullian and Origen and was confirmed in AD 300, when the Council of Elvira decreed that a woman who had an abortion should be refused the Sacrament.

With Augustine in the fourth century there came a change, for he contended that the soul came into existence not at birth but when the mother felt a movement or quickening within her. This was developed later by Aquinas, who postulated that the soul entered the foetus 40 days after conception. He regarded abortion before this 'ensoulment' as less serious, but thought it should still be condemned.[6] This view stemmed from Aristotle, who taught that new life did not become distinctly human until it was formed into a human shape by the animating principle of the soul. Thus a distinction was made between the formed foetus and the unformed. In 1591 Pope Gregory XIV confirmed this view, restricting penalties to those abortions carried out after the initial 40-day period. The common law in England reflected this Church view and allowed therapeutic abortion before ensoulment.[7] But this more liberal approach was set aside by Pope Innocent XI in 1679. In 1869 Pope Pius IX laid down the present Catholic position by insisting that human life began at conception. This removed any distinction between the formed and unformed foetus.

This shows that the Church has not been unanimous in its understanding of the moral status of the foetus. This issue is still debated today. Many Catholics, faced with particularly difficult situations, do have abortions, despite the teaching of their church. Moreover, some Catholic theologians contend that the present position is not in accord with tradition. When the mother's life is threatened the Catholic Church allows abortion. The principle of double effect which we have noted with respect to euthanasia works in this way with abortion. A surgeon may remove a cancerous uterus. This is his direct intention, but it results in the death of the foetus, which is foreseen but not intended. A utilitarian would accept this, for the operation has resulted in a good effect – namely, the saving of the mother's life. But the principle runs into difficulty when a direct killing of the foetus is required – that is to say, when the head of the foetus has to be crushed. This appears not to be acceptable to the Catholic Church even when the mother's life is at stake. In the case of rape an immediate curettage (a scraping of the uterus) is allowed. Killing, when it takes place in this context, is regarded as a necessary evil, and it must be shown that it has been done to avert a greater evil. Such a principle, while useful when a mother's life is at stake, could open the door to the argument that killing is sometimes necessary to avert other and greater evils.

It is no wonder that in a church of such variety of belief as the Anglican Church there are differences of view. The Church of England recognises that there are those, stressing the sanctity of life, who hold that the embryo deserves total protection, and that there are others who say that out of compassion towards the mother, termination of a pregnancy should be allowed for most reasons. However, the church holds that abortion is an evil, since every life is created in the divine image, and that abortion on demand is not permissible since it denies that truth. But the church agrees with abortion if there is a risk of a deformed child, if conception happens as a result of rape, and if the total bearing and rearing of the child would be beyond the total capacity of the mother. The Board of Social Responsibility of the Church does recognise that there is a failure medically to distinguish between the client's wishes and her needs, and that abortion on the scale of today calls into question the transcendent value of human life to which Christians are committed and to which our society in principle still subscribes. The Board is not satisfied with the working of the 1967 Act and gave support to David Alton's Bill to reduce the number of weeks at which abortion can be carried out from 28 to 18.

The Church of Scotland agrees that the Act is somewhat permissive and needs changing, particularly with regard to what has been called the social clause. It has called for greater effort to encourage mothers who feel that they cannot cope to consider adoption. The church has also emphasised the need for medical staff to be able to opt out of abortion work without prejudice to their careers. On the status of the foetus the church has argued that it is a human being from conception, made in the image of God, and that therefore it should be aborted only in the most serious of situations, such as a threat to the mother's life. There was much discussion in the Assembly over rape cases. Could the need to relieve the suffering of the mother justify the termination of the life of the foetus? Since it was contended that the foetus was a person from implantation in the womb, it was on the basis of an equality that the debate proceeded. All felt that the time limit for abortions should be reduced to at most twenty weeks. A significant figure was produced regarding abortions in Scotland which gave great cause for concern – namely, that 96.3 per cent were carried out under the Act's clause of danger to the physical or mental health of the mother, but only 1.6 per cent were due to some abnormality in the foetus. The Assembly felt that these figures represented an abuse of the Act, since reasons for abortions ranged from a girl being abandoned by her boyfriend to pregnancy interrupting a woman's career.

The United Reformed Church in England published a discussion paper on the subject in 1977. This noted an encouraging development in early abortions but expressed concern that private clinics were making excessive profits by offering abortion on request with scant counselling of the mother. Further, there is a major problem in the interpretation of the Act. In introducing the Bill, David Steel said, 'It is not the intention of the promotion of the Bill to leave a wide open door for abortion on request', but it has since become clear that abortion on request is in fact available to women who can pay. And since it is apparently a medical fact that continuing pregnancy to full term involves a greater risk to the woman's life and physical health than a reasonably early abortion the Steel Bill in fact legalises abortion on request. The United Reformed Church holds to the principle of reverence for life and therefore opposes abortion for reasons of social convenience, abortion on demand and abortion as a form of contraception. The Methodist and Baptist Churches reflected similar views in their own deliberations.

It is difficult to know the position of the American

Churches, apart from the basic opposition of fundamen-
talist groups, since there is much diversity. In general we
can say that Lutherans, Methodists and Episcopalians are
more liberal about abortion than Baptists and Catholics.
There is no official Baptist position but it is likely that they
would allow it when pregnancy was involuntary or in cases
of foetal deformity or cases where family reasons justified
it. And, while the Catholic Church continues the firm stand
which we have noted, a Gallup poll in 1992 reported that
Catholics thought that abortion should be legal in many or
all circumstances.[8] The Catholic Church has difficulties also
with contraception which is regarded as a form of abortion.
This surfaced in Kosovo in 1999 when the Vatican condemned the distribution of morning-after pills to rape
victims. Many insisted that the stand of the Church was
inhuman and demanded that the Vatican be thrown out of
the UN for abusing its position as an observer.

When we consider the teaching of Scripture there is not
much direct help in this difficult matter. In the Old Testament there is the command not to murder and not to cause
the death of the innocent (Exodus 23:7). The only text
pertaining to abortion refers to an accidental miscarriage
(Exodus 21:22). Theologians have debated the question of
the entry of the soul into the body, but have differed in
their views. There is difficulty in defining the term 'soul'.
Indeed, some hold that we cannot separate body and
soul, since the soul is the body's life factor. In short, there
is no certainty regarding the relation of the soul to the
embryo or the moment when such a relationship might
begin. In the New Testament there are passages which
regard the foetus in the womb as precious (Luke 1:42). In
connection with the birth of Jesus and John, Luke uses the
Greek word *brephos* (which means 'infant') to describe
both the foetus in the womb (1:44) and the new-born babe

(2:12). An alternative word could have been used for the former if he had wanted to distinguish it from the latter.

But if we regard the essence of Christianity as love (*agape*) we can approach the matter on a broader basis. We have seen in the article by Thomson her recognition of charity or love as well as justice. Now an interesting bringing together of the concepts of justice and love has been made by Joseph Fletcher in his book, *Moral Responsibility* (1967). Justice is giving everyone their due, but according to Christianity the one thing due to everyone is love; hence love and justice are the same. Justice, in the case of abortion, will have to see to it that love is applied to both mother and foetus – that is, unless we regard the foetus as a thing. Sometimes in the debate about its status in philosophical circles it appears to be just that. If it is there as a result of *eros* (lust), then little love may be shown towards it and its termination may be desired. But if it is a result of true love, then it is quite likely that the couple will be willing to accept responsibility for it. Love, according to 1 Corinthians, accepts responsibility; it is, in the Kantian terminology, good will. The highest ideal in Greek ethics following Aristotle was self-realisation, but Christian love is selfless. It is willing to suffer and still be kind and tries to endure all things. In very difficult circumstances the mother really becomes the Good Samaritan, even willing to risk her life for the sake of the innocent life which has been conceived.

Love is concerned with people, not things, and when there is doubt, as in abortion, whether the foetus is a person or not, it gives it the benefit. Love would not want to be wrong or have a guilt feeling or cause a harm which would be irreversible. Bernard Williams says that the experiences of a woman concerning abortion are the only thing that counts as a realistic and honest guide. There is evidence of many saying things like this:

— 'Afterwards I just could not get over it.'
— 'I hated myself for having an abortion.'
— 'How could I have ended a life?'
— 'I felt damaged by it.'
— 'There was no sense of joy or relief.'

The Christian ideal of *agape* may, however, seem somewhat idealistic to many in our secular scene. But there is evidence that some of the greatest non-Christians have been impressed by it. As Bertrand Russell said, 'What the world needs is Christian love or compassion.'[9]

WHAT ABOUT THE LAW?

The principles we have mentioned may influence decisions, but in the context of rival claims and rights they need to be flexible and informed by compassion. As we have seen, controversy rages over when the foetus is to be regarded as a person, and there does not seem to be any end to it. Yet much moral philosophy and the 1967 Act support the view that becoming a person is a gradual process and that therefore rights accompany this growth. What remains to be decided is where the crucial point of viability is, and it comes as a surprise to discover that Britain is out of line here with other European countries. No other country in Western Europe permits abortion as late as 24 weeks; the average limit is 12 to 14 weeks. This appears more in accord with the physical development of the foetus in the womb as we have described it. No wonder that since 1967 there have been attempts to get the law changed in the UK. Moreover, there is evidence to show reluctance on the part of doctors to perform operations in the time span envisaged by the Act. In 1986 there were 2,723 legal abortions after 20 weeks but only 29 after 24 weeks.

However, what happens in the UK legally is very likely to be influenced not only by Europe but also by America, which has moved from the conferring of legal rights on 'unborn children' to the granting of the right of a woman to have an abortion in the first and second trimesters of pregnancy (a trimester is three months). This happened because of a now-famous case which concerned the abortion laws of Texas, where legal abortions had been restricted to those deemed necessary to save the woman's life.

The case was the subject of a film which appeared on British TV. A young woman, who in the film had the fictitious name of Jane Roe, challenged various Texan laws relating to abortion and succeeded in getting them declared unconstitutional. She appeared in the film as a somewhat light-headed person who became pregnant quite frequently. This was her second pregnancy, and she realised that she couldn't properly care for the baby. Indeed, the first baby was currently being looked after by her mother, whose relationship with her daughter was anything but sympathetic! The pregnancies had resulted from intercourse with two different men. Jane Roe said that the father of the child she was now carrying had no interest in it; indeed, he did not appear in the film at all. Her position resembled that of many girls in the States, whose recurring pregnancies were unwanted for a variety of reasons, such as inconvenience, family planning, economics, dislike of children, illegitimacy, and so on.

Faced with the rigidity of the Texas laws, she thought there might be a loophole if she said that she had been raped. But the legal advice was that this would be difficult to sustain, so the case was based on a woman's right to privacy which, broadly interpreted, meant the right to be left alone to make her own decision freely. In the event the Texas statutes were declared to be unconstitutional in the state court, but Jane Roe was not granted an injunction for an abortion. It took some time for the case to go to the Supreme Court, and in the meantime Jane had the baby, which was adopted. In the film it appeared that she received little economic help or proper counselling, and one scene showed that even her defence lawyer did not know she had had the baby! If this is a correct portrayal of what happened it is no wonder that at one point she attempted to commit suicide. In 1973 the Supreme Court ruled that a woman's right to terminate a pregnancy was not absolute, but since the meaning of the word 'person' does not include the 'unborn', a woman may have an abortion for a variety of reasons. However, the court did stress the protection of the potential life of the foetus. During the first trimester the decision to have an abortion will be taken by the doctor in consultation with his patient, and the State will not interfere. At other stages the state may prevent an abortion taking place if it judges that the reason is not a good one.

There was much criticism of the Supreme Court ruling, and there was increasing pressure to revise the law in a country where abortion has become a most divisive issue. If the potential for life as a person is there from conception, how can the foetus be of less value in the early stages of its development than in the later stages? Only if one accepts the sliding scale of growth and rights which we have noted. Does the decision to abort not place too much responsibility on the medical profession, and do not physicians differ greatly on what justifies it? Was not the Supreme Court inconsistent in saying that it did not know when life begins but then proceeding to resolve the problem by saying that it could 'prescribe' abortion after the first and second trimester? Daniel Callagan sees the danger of leaving matters on an existential basis in which freedom of individual choice and conscience is the dominant factor. He writes: 'I have always found that an odd kind of contention, one which, if followed rigorously, would leave all decisions bearing on the concepts of "justice", "equality", the "general welfare", and the like, up to the individual consciences.'[10]

A wave of moral protest against the Roe v. Wade decision swept America. The issue centres on the question of individual liberty and state regulative control. In response, Ronald Reagan, when he came to office, replaced some of the members of the Supreme Court with pro-life people, and in 1989 the Court ruled that the various states of the union would decide what regulations would govern abortion. Such decisions should emerge in the future. In the meantime the clash between pro-abortion and anti-abortion groups in America has been graphically depicted on TV in this country. Women seeking an abortion have been shown with their heads covered, surrounded by escorts, being pressurised by anti-abortionists trying to make them change their minds. As such pressure for and against mounts in the various states, violence could ensue and pose a problem for the security forces. Politicians are being elected on this issue alone, and economic and social problems are being pushed into the background. President Bush supported Reagan's point of view, saying that the Roe v. Wade decision was a tragedy and must be altered. Clinton, however, took a more liberal line than his predecessors, as might be expected of someone who has had sexual misconduct problems. The whole debate is being conducted in a very emotional atmosphere. The pro-abortionists are promoting the freedom of the individual woman over against any regulation. In a reassessment, the Supreme Court declined explicitly to overturn Roe v. Wade but in effect invited the 50 state legislatures to decide for themselves.

A legal event of significance occurred in Britain in April 1990, when in the House of Commons the questions of research on embryos and abortion were discussed. It was decided to amend the Abortion Act of 1967 so as to limit abortion to 24 weeks instead of 28. But no time limit was set for abortions necessary because of possible injury to the physical or mental health of the mother. Anti-abortionists welcomed the restricted time limit but were disappointed that they had not got 18 weeks. The Catholic Church, in a statement by Cardinal Basil Hume, expressed its dissent and argued that the amendments would lead to late terminations. Catholics wanted the government to move towards amendments to the Bill which would make the 24-week limit apply to all abortions, including those cases where pregnancy might produce a handicapped child or damage the health of the mother.

But it was noted in the debate that in 1988 only 22 abortions were performed after the twenty-fourth week out of an annual total of 183,000. What concerns the churches and the anti-abortionists in general is the reasons for such abortions. They believe that while abortion is not permissible on demand, it is often being carried out when the defects in the foetus are not serious or when there is little likelihood of pregnancy causing real harm to the mother. It is estimated that every year Britain carries out more than 2,000 abortions when the foetus is not abnormal.

IN VITRO FERTILISATION AND RESEARCH ON EMBRYOS

In vitro fertilisation (IVF), with its 'test-tube babies' and growing of embryos in laboratories for the purpose of research, has a bearing on abortion, for it raises again the question of the moral status of the foetus and embryo. The technique does bring happiness to infertile couples. An egg is extracted from the womb and the semen of the husband or donor is mixed in. The fertilised egg is then transferred to the mother's uterus. The next step is the implantation of the embryo in the uterine wall. In 1978 we had the first 'test-tube baby', and now we have superovulation. This produces a number of eggs and so increases the chances of successful pregnancy. There would be a danger of a multiple pregnancy if all the eggs were transferred, so three is regarded as the maximum. But this raises the problem of what to do with the surplus eggs. Should they be transferred to a woman who cannot produce her own eggs or should they be used for research? We return to this problem later.

If the husband's semen is not fertile it may be necessary to use a donor. This is artificial insemination by donor (AID) rather than IVF. It is condemned by the churches and by others who see this as an intervention of a third party into a marriage relationship. It also presents problems for the couple, since the child will not have a genetic relation to the husband of the marriage. Conversely, if the woman cannot produce an egg, one may be donated, fertilised with her husband's semen and then transferred to her uterus. This has the same difficulties.

If the embryo is seen as a person or human being from conception, all research is ruled out, but those who accept a sliding scale of values with regard to its development have no problems in this respect. Since nature itself destroys about 60 per cent of embryos and miscarriages and preventions of birth are brought about by artificial methods, perhaps we are placing too much value on this early stage of life and research is quite in order. Norman Autton remarks: 'Early embryos are capable, like sperm, ova and corpses, but unlike developed foetuses, babies and adults, of deep freezing. If the conceptus is seen as already human life, not to be discarded or altered destructively, what kind of life is it that can thus be arrested?'[11]

The Warnock Report recommended that the embryo should be protected by law, that research should be permitted only under licence and that the embryo should not be used as a research subject after fourteen days from fertilisation. Research requires the permission of the parents, and embryos which have been experimented on should never be implanted in a mother. The intention of the researcher is important, and this is acceptable if it is directed towards resolving problems of infertility or abnormality.

The same attitude to research was evident when the debate took place at the House of Commons in April 1990. As a result it was decided to confirm the fourteen-day limit laid down by the Warnock Report and to stipulate that experiments on human cloning and the creation of human/animal hybrids must not take place. The House of Lords had already backed research on embryos by a majority of three to one. The archbishops and bishops of the Church of England supported research on the basis of the fourteen-day limit, but as we have already noted, the Catholic Church was not satisfied with the result of the debate, believing that it was a liberalisation of both research and abortion.

CONCLUSION

Abortion is a serious matter and cannot be undertaken for trivial reasons, for here we are dealing with life in its most unprotected form. Those who have undertaken the decision without much thought have regretted it in later life. Unfortunately it is inevitable that we are called upon to make crucial decisions affecting our career, marriage and parenthood early in life, when we have not gained sufficient wisdom to make them wisely. And it is hard, not only in youth but also in old age, to avoid self-interest and even callousness in many of the decisions we make.

While life is intrinsically valuable, being the most precious thing that we have got, abortion where the child is likely to be born with a severe handicap or where the mother's life or mental health is in danger appears acceptable. Difficulty arises over determining the gravity of the handicap, but it would seem wrong to withhold treatment from a Down's syndrome baby, since these children can live quite happy lives. The problem here is really a social one, since rearing such a child is very difficult. But if we are to concern ourselves not only with the mother's problems but also with the best interests of the child, then such children should not be aborted or allowed to die.

There is disquiet about abortions being carried out for social and economic reasons. Should disruption of the lifestyle of the mother and family or the fact that another child will be a burden or the necessity of giving up a job for a while or the social disgrace of an illegitimate birth be sufficient reasons for an abortion? These are serious concerns, but if the baby is not wanted there is always the possibility of doing a very worthwhile thing by giving birth to it and having it adopted. Anyone who has seen the joy on the faces of adoptive parents when they have received such a baby will agree that something marvellous has been done for them. Some argue that the effect on the mother of carrying a baby to term and then having to part with it is more traumatic than that of abortion. But we have noted the many who regret abortion; moreover, little study has been done to compare the different effects on a woman of having an abortion and having the baby adopted. We would need to know more about these effects before making a judgement.

As we have noted, one of the most debatable matters is when an abortion should take place. The limit in Britain now is 24 weeks. This corresponds with the United States but is not in line with the other EEC countries, where the average upper limit is 12–14 weeks.

The American and British decision rests on viability, which is the foetus' ability to exist independent of the mother. In some ways this is odd, for babies are not independent and require much love and care. The decision centres around the idea that independence means the ability to breathe, but new technology could push the timing further back. Morality cannot be based on technology, though what the former allows is influenced by the latter. Thus some thinkers argue on moral or religious grounds that conception is the only acceptable time limit, while others argue for a limit much later than 24 weeks. In the light of our discussion, what time limit can we argue for?

There are good reasons for the time limit of 12–14 weeks which has been set by the EEC countries, but we need to remember that during this period they are as liberal as the United States in granting abortion on demand. Within its 24-week period Britain is less liberal. Then there is the fact that the Christian tradition is not unanimous on the question of when an abortion may take place. The Warnock Report may also have an implication for abortion which is often overlooked. If research on embryos is limited to the 14 days after fertilisation, does this not indicate a value given to the embryo after that time? As Anthony Kenny says: 'All the reasons put forward by the Warnock Committee for prohibiting experimentation on embryos after the fourteenth day seem to be equally good reasons for prohibiting the destruction of embryos and the abortion of foetuses after that day also.'[12] What the Report does is to inculcate moral respect for the embryo and make us think seriously about its further development. In this development human qualities begin to show quite early. From the fifth week the divisions of the brain can be seen, and by the end of the eighth week most of the human body parts are present and the lower brain anatomy is well developed. In the previous chapter we noted that death is connected with the brain. If this is so, we might say that life begins when the brain exists or when it begins to function. If we were to accept this, we would have to say that the time limit for abortion should be eight weeks rather than twenty-four. The brain is significant in this connection because it gives us our capacity for thought, which distinguishes us from the animals. In contrast, some authorities on the subject take the view that the foetus is viable when it has the ability to breathe. But why should this take precedence over thinking and feeling? Foetal brain activity comes after lung development and occurs at around 24 weeks. Significantly, criteria drawn from brain activity and those drawn from viability coincide regarding the time factor, but the former rest on moral value rather than any question of physical independence.[13]

Yet there are problems with the brain criteria. It is difficult to know when brain stimulus begins. With some embryos and foetuses it has been recorded at eight weeks; with others it is later. Can we base our criteria for a time limit on abortion on the speed of brain development? But taking all these viewpoints together, we can conclude that an abortion should take place as soon as possible after conception. This is confirmed by the experience of women themselves, and it is such experience which must be a major factor in our thinking about this serious matter. Early abortion is less emotionally stressful for women, medically easier and less likely to involve post-operative complications. The foetus is less developed, as we have seen, and the operation can be carried out quickly. This enables the mother to leave the hospital sooner and thereby releases a bed for another patient. When Harriet Harman was Shadow Health Minister, she pointed in this connection to a survey carried out by the Royal College of Obstetricians and Gynaecologists. It shows that of every five women who have an abortion after twenty weeks, one asked to have it before the twelfth week of pregnancy. The eight weeks of delay was caused by red tape and lack of services. One of the most urgent needs is for more money for district health authorities so that they can prevent ward closures and provide more guidance and help for women faced with this grave decision.

In an ideal world there would be few abortions, for there would be no unwanted children. But both Christian and non-Christian agree that this is not an ideal world. The Christian ethic calls for restraint in a sexually permissive world. There are signs that the younger generation are beginning to adopt such an attitude, if not for Christian reasons, then because of self-interest. But such restraint cannot be imposed. We live in a secular and pluralistic society, and the debate about abortion with its many different viewpoints, reflects this fact. But while there is disagreement, we can all extend help, love, sympathy and understanding when a woman is faced with the choice of whether to have an abortion or not. This is in the tradition of the Good Samaritan.[14]

Questions for discussion
• Distinguish the different views on the moral status of the foetus. What do you favour?

- Can utilitarianism give a plausible account of the rights and wrongs of abortion?
- The foetus is not a person therefore abortion is morally innocuous. Do you agree?
- Since a woman has a right to control her own body it is always morally permissible for her to have an abortion?

FOUR

The Ultimate Penalty

On the morning of 13 July 1955 Ruth Ellis was hanged in Holloway Prison. She had become pregnant by a young man, but he had then wanted to break off the affair. In a violent argument between them he had struck her in the abdomen, causing her to miscarry. Enraged by the assault, she shot him dead as he came out of a public house in Hampstead. Instead of recognising provocation, the court refused a manslaughter verdict and brought in a sentence of death. There was enormous public outcry with demonstrations, letters to the newspapers and nightly vigils outside the prison. The case was covered by the media worldwide.

It was cases like this and others where there was some doubt about the guilt of the condemned that strengthened the movement against the death penalty in England and resulted in its abolition in 1965. It was reported in the mid-1990s that 54 countries had abolished the death penalty, 15 only held it for exceptional crimes such as wartime crimes and those 27 countries which retained it had not executed anyone for 10 years. An interesting case developed in 1999 in the Caribbean. Nine drug dealers who had committed murder were condemned to hang but the Privy Council in London intervened to save them from the noose.

The Council was Trinidad's final court of appeal due to a quirk of post-colonial law. Trinidad insisted that Britain was living with moral uncertainty and has lost the values which it imposed on them! Such values insist that the punishment must fit the crime. Of the criminals' guilt there was no doubt for one of the killers turned state witness and was subsequently shot by them. The Caribbean community demanded that the Privy Council be replaced by their own Caribbean Court of Appeal.

In the next two sections we want to state some of the arguments for and against capital punishment and then go on to offer some comment on their strengths and weaknesses.

ARGUMENTS FOR CAPITAL PUNISHMENT

It is argued that some crimes deserve death, and that they are not justly punished if it is not inflicted. By carrying out such acts of violence criminals choose such a punishment for themselves. Philip Hope-Wallace describes such a crime and his reactions to it. He knew a girl who was a fine historian on the threshold of her career. She was somewhat shy, but sensible and charming. She was a good daughter, and on one occasion she took her mother to a resort in Europe for a holiday. After lunch one day she went for a stroll alone above the town. There she was clubbed, raped, held captive in a cave and after some time bludgeoned to death. Hope-Wallace said that when he heard this story his liberal abolitionist scruples flew into fragments. Although he remained against the universal application of the death penalty, he felt that there were crimes where just retribution was appropriate.

Retribution is a key word in any defence of the death penalty. It is maintained that retribution is not the same thing as revenge, for that is personal. Such an emotion does not enter into the process of justice. Further, some crimes are so awful that only the ultimate penalty of death can be appropriate to them. It is a lawful requital for the suffering inflicted upon the victim. Since the law is grounded in the principle of equality, the murderer must be paid back in kind.

The relation of a person to society should be understood in the matter of retribution. Both Thomas Hobbes and John Locke influenced the writing of the United States constitution and they argued that in forming societies men and women entered into a social contract whereby they conceded certain natural rights. The rules of such a society must be accompanied by sanctions that fit the crime, and murder is the worst. If someone takes another's life he forfeits the right to participate in society, therefore life imprisonment is insufficient.

Immanuel Kant agreed and said that we must look back at the crime which has been committed and realise that the balance of justice has been disturbed and must be set right. The criminal draws the deed back upon himself and expiates his crime by death. As we have seen in previous chapters, Kant opposes the idea of making use of people as a means rather than an end, and this is what the criminal has done. He has murdered to achieve an end, believing that the end justified the means. But we must respect people and regard their lives as sacred, no matter what we may feel about them or what desires or ends we may have in mind. We act with respect towards other people because of our common humanity and reason, not because of love or inclination. The one good thing in the world is the 'good will' which ensures that we act on the basis of duty and have respect for the life of each individual member of the community. Kant is really repeating the Golden Rule: 'Do unto others as you would have them do unto you.'[1]

Kant would have been opposed, therefore, to the utilitarian argument which often figures in House of Commons debates concerning capital punishment. That argument says that if the death penalty is to be used, it must be to deter others from committing the crime of murder. Many Members of Parliament still argue on these grounds and the view is also expressed by the police and the public in general.

How far, then, can it be ascertained by empirical research that the death penalty does deter criminals from murder? Those who are for the death penalty can point to various projects which have established that it does have a deterrent effect. To give one example, Isaac Ehrlich, an economist, used a statistical method known as 'regression analysis' to examine the possible effect of executions and other variables on homicides in the USA as a whole between 1932 and 1970. During that period, and especially in the 1960s, homicides increased while executions declined. Ehrlich therefore concluded that deterrence did exist and suggested that 'an additional execution per year over the period in question may have resulted, on average, in 7 or 8 fewer murders'.[2] But other studies, as we will see in the next section, dispute this finding.

Utilitarians, while they are committed to the spread of happiness, can justify capital punishment on the ground that the suffering of one may benefit the many. So if capital punishment does deter it should be carried out.

Jeremy Bentham believed that hanging should be a public spectacle that all could observe so that terror might be struck into their hearts. John Stuart Mill, in the debate in the House of Commons in 1868, argued that the death penalty should be administered for aggravated murder. He said it was 'the least cruel mode in which it was possible adequately to deter from crime'. He also resorted to retribution as a justification for it:

> When there has been brought home to any one, by conclusive evidence, the greatest crime known to the law; and then the attendant circumstances suggest no palliation of the guilt, no hope that the culprit may even yet not be unworthy to live among mankind, nothing to make it probable that the crime was an exception to his general character rather than a consequence of it, then I confess it appears to me that to deprive the criminal of the life of which he has proved himself unworthy – solemnly to blot him out from the fellowship of mankind and from the catalogue of the living – is the most appropriate, as it is certainly the most impressive, mode in which society can attach to so great a crime the penal consequences which for the security of life it is indispensable to annex to it.[3]

Mill goes on to say that such a penalty is actually what he calls 'humanity to the criminal' or benefit to him. Some proponents of capital punishment argue that a life sentence is worse than death, considering the isolation and deprivation of the prison cells.

A further argument that is advanced is that the people want capital punishment. Public opinion polls in the USA since 1960 have shown this, and there is some evidence in the UK, especially after a particularly vicious crime has taken place, that the people would support the bringing back of the death penalty.[4]

The alternative to the death penalty is life imprisonment. This may be commuted because of good behaviour, but there is no guarantee that the killer will not kill again. There have been lifers who have killed prison warders while in prison and escapees who have been involved in further attempts at killing. Pope John Paul II was shot by Mehmet Ali Agca, an escapee from a Turkish prison who had been convicted of murder; and Laron Williams, after his escape from a Memphis prison, was charged with a fresh murder. Jack Henry Abbot, an imprisoned murderer, admitted to committing another murder after his parole from prison; and Joseph Bowen, sentenced in 1971 for the murder of a policeman, was convicted in 1975 of the murder of a prison warder and his deputy. He is reported to have 'laughed when he heard himself sentenced to two life terms'. On 29 October 1981 he led several prison inmates in the taking of 38 hostages. R. Berger, in citing these examples drawn from various sources, notes that life imprisonment does not mean lifelong imprisonment at all, and cannot offer complete protection to society.[5] Those who campaign for the death penalty acknowledge that the number of second murders committed by those already convicted is small, but argue that this risk must be taken into account.

ARGUMENTS AGAINST CAPITAL PUNISHMENT

Amnesty International argues against the death penalty on the ground that it is a cruel, inhuman and degrading punishment and violates the right to life. It is used as an instrument of repression against political opposition and against racial, ethnic, religious and underprivileged groups. It is an act of violence which tends to provoke violence. It has not been shown to have a deterrent effect and is brutalising to all who are involved in the process.

Further, execution can be inflicted on the innocent. Amnesty International's report *When the State Kills* (1989) points out that a study published in 1987 cited 349 US cases between 1900 and 1985 in which innocent people were wrongly convicted of crimes punishable by death; 23 of them were executed. And since 1985 at least two prisoners who may have been innocent have been executed. Willie Jasper Darden was executed in Florida on 15 March 1988 despite evidence from two independent alibi witnesses suggesting that he could not have been at the scene of the crime when the murder was committed. Another was Edward Earl Johnson (a black man), executed in Mississippi on 20 May 1987 for the murder of a white police officer. Following Johnson's arrest, an eyewitness to the crime (who knew him personally) at first told the police that he was not the assailant. Johnson, who always maintained that he was innocent, alleged that the police had threatened and coerced him into signing a confession, on the basis of which he was sentenced to death. Since his execution, an alibi witness has stated that she was with him at a pool hall during the time when the murder was committed.[6]

In the UK doubts have been raised about the guilt of prisoners hanged in the past. One such case is that of James Hanratty, who was in 1962 sentenced to death for the murder of Michael Gregsten (this was known as 'the A6 murder'). More recently, if the death penalty had been operative the Birmingham Six and the Guildford Four could have been subjected to it; but they were released. All were convicted of IRA bomb attacks. During a debate on the death penalty in the House of Commons in April 1987, Roy Jenkins, a former Home Secretary, said, 'I had to deal with 10 capital cases in which there were varying degrees of doubt, some quite simply amounting to wrongful conviction.' Not all the prisoners were hanged, 'but two were, and more would have been had the death penalty not been abolished in 1965'. He said, 'It is my view that the frailty of human judgment . . . is too great to support the finality of capital punishment.'[7] Some go further and contend that juries who have condemned an innocent man should themselves be tried for murder.

The southern states of the USA are known for their continuance of the death penalty. There is evidence of miscarriage of justice and prejudice against blacks. They belong to the poorer section of the community and cannot hire the skilled lawyers to defend them that the whites can. Statistics show that more blacks are executed for murder than whites who are guilty of similar crimes. Perhaps this was one of the reasons – apart from viewing the death penalty as a cruel and unusual punishment – why the Supreme Court of the USA suspended all death sentences in 1972. But in 1976 it declared them to be constitutional.

Yet doubt was raised about the nature of this punishment. It was argued that it was a barbaric ritual pandering to the lowest instincts of humanity and that it had a brutalising effect on those who took part and witnessed it. Attention was focused on the physical and mental effect on prisoners waiting on 'death row' for execution. It was maintained that capital punishment is premeditated murder and cannot be compared to any criminal act. To be equivalent the criminal would have had to warn his victim, whom he had imprisoned, at what date he intended to kill him.

The argument that the death penalty deters cannot be sustained. Isaac Ehrlich's research, which we noted in the last section, has been criticised on methodological grounds. He omitted factors such as the increasing availability of guns and the fact that while crimes in general had increased during the 1960s, the increase in the number of homicides was less than that of other crimes against the person.

Thorsten Sellin carried out research for the Model Penal Code Project of the American Law Institute and concluded that executions have no discernible effect on homicide death rates. Needless to say, Isaac Ehrlich did not agree with his methods. But, having considered the work of these researchers and others, the National Academy of Sciences in 1975 stated that 'the deterrent effect of capital punishment is definitely not a settled matter and this is the strongest social scientific conclusion that can be reached at the present time'.[8] If no benefit can be proven, then the death penalty should not be imposed.

The death penalty is final and cuts off any hope of reforming the prisoner and reclaiming him for society. The right to life is a supreme right. Further, execution may be seen by political groups as martyrdom and so may actually encourage violent crime. This is one of the reasons why the UK government refused to bring back the death penalty for members of the IRA convicted of murder.

When the death penalty is in operation in any country it could result in murderers going free because juries are frightened of the possibility of condemning an innocent person to death. Moreover, the state, in taking the life of a criminal, is violating the principle of the sacredness of life. Payment is due for the crime but justice does not require that a bad means – execution – be used to a good end – just punishment. Only God has the right to take life, since he gave it. This is laid down in the commandment not to kill.

Before commenting on these arguments we will look at Christian arguments which have had an influence on the laws of many countries.

THE CHRISTIAN PERSPECTIVE

The Hebrew religion from which Christianity sprang administered the death penalty for all kinds of crime: witchcraft, blasphemy, failure to keep the Sabbath, murder, rape, adultery, kidnapping and so on. In particular, murder was stressed in the sixth commandment, 'Thou shalt not kill'. This is not only the teaching of the Pentateuch (the first five books of the Old Testament, traditionally ascribed to Moses) but also that of the prophetic writings as well. The commandment was based on the principle of the sanctity of life. Retribution was stressed in the statement, 'Whoever sheds the blood of man, by man shall his blood be shed; for God made man in his own image' (Genesis 9:6, RSV). Various methods of execution were used, including stoning, burning, beheading and strangling.

Various limitations, however, were placed upon the death penalty. Thus, in the case of manslaughter, where killing was an accident or not intended or the result of a blow, the death penalty was not enforced. Cities of refuge were founded where the offender could flee so that there might be time to investigate fully the circumstances of his crime. Motive and intention were given a high priority in dealing with such cases. The condemnation of the murderer was very difficult to obtain and the death penalty was rarely invoked. But when it did happen an attempt was made to deter others by making the execution as public as possible. The body was left hanging on the gibbet for an entire day.

When Christianity emerged in the first century AD Palestine was occupied by the Romans, so the Jews could not carry out the death penalty themselves. But the Sanhedrin, the Supreme Court of the Jews, had jurisdiction over all religious and theological concerns and, according to the Gospels, they passed the sentence of death on Jesus for blasphemy. This sentence had to be endorsed by their conquerors and only they could carry it out. Such a religious charge would not have impressed the Roman governor Pilate, so the Sanhedrin charged Jesus with political agitation, trying to get the people not to pay tribute to Caesar and assuming the title of King. Most commentators consider these charges unjust, but the point that we are interested in is that the Jews still believed that the death penalty should be used. After the fall of the Jewish Temple in AD 70 the Jews in their subsequent history had to live by the laws of the countries where they dwelt. The new state of Israel was founded in 1948, and it abandoned the death penalty in 1954, except for treason in wartime and for Nazis who had committed crimes against the Jews.

Jesus taught that there should not be retaliation or retribution in the relations between men and women but did not comment on how a state should handle murderers. There is no specific condemnation of the death penalty in the New Testament. Paul recognises that the state has been given the power to take 'retribution on the offender' but he does not say what penalty should be administered for murder (Romans 13:2-5).

Later we shall look at the one story in the New Testament where Jesus was asked about his attitude to the crime of adultery, for which the Jewish law demanded the death penalty.

As the tradition of the Church developed, early Fathers such as Tertullian and Origen opposed capital punishment, but Augustine in the fourth century defended it on the ground that the Old Testament commanded it. The Church appears from that time onwards to have believed this. In the Middle Ages, when it was troubled by heretics, it burnt them at the stake. In the sixteenth century the Protestant Reformers Martin Luther and John Calvin, while denying much that the Church then believed about salvation, agreed with the death penalty. Luther said that the ruler and the hangman were striking a blow for God against the devil, and Calvin concurred with this verdict. This attitude had a powerful influence in Europe, in Britain and eventually in the USA. However, in more recent times churches have usually adopted the abolitionists' view.

The Church of England sees the death penalty as containing vengeance and as not being compatible with effecting a criminal's moral restoration. Forgiveness, love and reclamation represent the Christian viewpoint, and retribution does not include the possibility of redemptive and remedial action. Archbishop Ramsey, speaking in the House of Lords debate in 1965, pointed this out and then went on to argue that the death penalty devalued human life. It meant society saying, in effect: 'This man has killed someone. Very well, we will kill him too.' But this did not enhance the sacredness of life; it diminished it further. Ramsey argued that a life sentence was a sufficient deterrent. Other bishops argued that vengeance belonged to God and that he would repay. They agreed with those arguments that stressed that people who were involved in the process of carrying through the death penalty were being degraded. Moreover, this degrading extended to society in general. Similar sentiments were expressed by representatives of the Church of England in 1969 when the House of Lords debated the continuation of the 1965 suspension of capital punishment, and again in 1977 when the Church's General Synod threw out a motion which would have reopened the question for the category of terrorist murders.

The United Reformed Church also opposes capital punishment. In conjunction with the Council of Churches for Britain and Ireland, during parliamentary debates on this issue it sends to MPs letters urging them not to vote in favour of the death penalty. However, in its course texts for the training of the laity it is careful in discussing retribution to show that in the context of penal policy, capital punishment does not mean vengeance or revenge. This is something which the Church of England needs to take note of in its contribution to the debate. The text says: 'For Christians down through the centuries the retributive tradition has been important because, assuming that people are properly convicted and responsible for their actions, punishment is a witness that they are being treated with due seriousness and respect as responsible human beings.'[9]

The other churches, while differing in many matters, are united in their opposition to the death penalty. The World Council of Churches reflected this attitude by joining with 42 international non-governmental organisations in submitting to the Sixth United Nations Congress on the Prevention of Crime and the Treatment of Offenders a statement which called for the abolition of the death penalty throughout the world.

The general attitude of Christianity which has developed is that punishment is necessary as a deterrent, and to show the criminal that crime does not pay and the law must be respected, and to effect a change in the lifestyle of the offender. 'Retribution', 'reform', 'remedial' – these words are now the basis of the Christian viewpoint. The overriding principle is love (*agape*) – not easy, sentimental emotion but the persevering desire for a person's good. Hence it is contended that administering the death penalty is an admission of failure; it is saying that society cannot change the person and that the grace of God is limited. The Christian viewpoint also emphasises that every effort should be made to turn our prisons from places of punishment into places where it is not retribution that is stressed but cure. Since Christians in the past have done a lot for prison reform, it is argued that they can be involved today and can work to make sure that no man or woman emerges from prison worse than they were when they went in. Sadly, prison often turns offenders into worse people.

COMMENTS ON THE ARGUMENTS

It is difficult to calculate the balance between the suffering of the victim and that of the murderer. Abolitionists stress that the death penalty is barbaric, but it is difficult to accept this when comparing it with the awfulness of some murders. Further, the victim is innocent unless it can be demonstrated that he had done something grievous to the murderer which could be interpreted as provocation. In this case the verdict would be manslaughter and questions about the death penalty would not arise. When a cold-blooded killer, who has planned a deliberate crime or who kills an innocent person whom he does not even know just for the fun of it, is shot by the police or executed there is not a rejection on the part of the public but an instinctive feeling that the killing is right. However, this is something which we will discuss more fully in the next section. What can be said regarding the argument that the death penalty is a cruel and unusual punishment, since it entails a long period of waiting on death row? Books have been written describing the awfulness of this and the feelings and anguish of criminals condemned to death. It has not been established, however, that the physical conditions are any worse than those experienced by other inmates of prisons.

The waiting period is observed partly out of concern that every chance should be given to the offender to appeal against the sentence. There can be little doubt that in the USA lawyers exploit every legal loophole to appeal against the capital conviction.

A TV film entitled *Death in the Onion Fields* describes how a police officer was murdered in cold blood by one of two criminals apprehended after a robbery. While waiting in prison both criminals met another who was well versed in legal practice and had learned every trick of the trade. He showed them how to appeal against their convictions. These appeals dragged on for years and eventually the two men escaped the death penalty and got life sentences. But sometimes the law drags its feet and subjects prisoners to a long wait on death row. Perhaps the period of waiting could be reduced as long as it does not prejudice the opportunity of an appeal.

If the category of murder to which the death penalty should be applied is narrowed down to aggravated murder only, the advocate appears to have a stronger case. And he can also point to the fact that certain countries which have abolished the death penalty for murder still retain capital punishment for other crimes. Hence it would simply be a matter of extending the scope of the death penalty. England retains such a penalty for high treason both in peacetime and in wartime under the Treason Act, 1919, and United Kingdom Crown Dependencies, Jersey and the Isle of Man retain the death penalty. But it is doubtful that the death penalty would be administered in the United Kingdom even for high treason, and any death sentences imposed in Jersey and the Isle of Man have been commuted by the Queen to life imprisonment.

The death penalty is often described as a cruel punishment and it is true that a study of the various methods used in the past could justify this judgement. But with reference to modern methods such as electrocution, firing squads and lethal injections the charge of cruelty is less convincing. In the case of lethal injections there is the problem of getting medical personnel involved. There has been opposition to such involvement from the World Medical Association and various other associations in different countries.

The argument that news of the carrying out of an execution excites world-wide attention and panders to the lowest instincts of humanity appears a strong one, especially in view of the tendency of some newspapers to create sensations rather than report them. But if the death penalty were administered by a lethal injection in the prisoner's cell, such an argument would be undercut. Of course, such an execution, not being public, would have little deterrent effect. But we have seen that the deterrence argument is empirically inconclusive, and therefore if the argument for the death sentence is to be carried there is need to rest it on retribution.

The arguments against the death penalty assume two matters: first that death is terrible and second that a life sentence is bound to be preferable. Both assumptions can be challenged.

In our discussion of euthanasia we have noticed that some philosophers argue for the right to die of patients suffering from painful diseases and have advocated giving them a lethal injection. Ironically, such thinkers appear to be opposed to the death penalty. Their arguments for euthanasia or active killing often rest on the ground that many patients will never have a 'worthwhile life' again. And yet it seems obvious that conditions in the jails often do not contribute to a worthwhile existence. If it were otherwise many jail riots in various countries might not have occurred.

Another point that we noted was the stress laid on choice, especially by existentialist philosophers. Thus in abortion cases it was argued that the mother had the right to choose and that this was a paramount factor. Why then should a prisoner not have the right to choose between death and a life sentence? Gary Gilmore decided that he had such a right to demand death, but had to go to great lengths to get it. He attempted suicide, but failed; then he went through a long process of trying to convince the State of Utah that he preferred death to life imprisonment. Only when the moratorium on state executions was lifted by the Supreme Court of the USA did Gilmore achieve his objective. He was executed by a firing squad in 1977.

What then should be said about the argument that the people want capital punishment? In a democracy this is a strong argument, but the majority may be ill informed and they may want the death sentence for the wrong reasons, such as vengeance or the desire to see someone suffering. Representatives in Parliament do not always see themselves as following the views of their constituents and may consider that they are better informed about the arguments for and against the death penalty.

One difficulty that confronts the normal person considering the motives and intentions of the criminal is that of trying to think the way he does. The assumption that is made by a number of writers is that he reasons and feels the way they do. But how can this be assumed? Is not the public's reaction of deep horror to the murder of a child or an elderly person proof that the majority of average people could not do such things in a premeditated way? But the criminal guilty of first degree murder has indeed done such a thing. If he is declared sane, how can we understand such a mentality? How can we be sure that for him the process of waiting for execution or the thought of the death penalty would be anything like what it would be for us? Perhaps the arguments based on the mental suffering of the condemned man may not be so strong after all.

Again, if the death penalty is so terrible, why does it not deter the criminal? Does he not have the same fear of death as we do? And, as we have mentioned, is it true that he fears the 'short pang of a rapid death' more than the 'living tomb' of a prison?

A stronger argument against the death penalty is the possibility of a miscarriage of justice. A utilitarian may not worry too much about this, either because such instances are rare, as J. S. Mill said, or because the suffering of the innocent may on occasion lead to the greatest happiness of the greatest number. This latter reason is not generally acceptable. If the death penalty were to be applied on a retributivist basis, juries would have to be beyond suspicion and the guilt of the criminal would have to be established beyond any reasonable doubt. At one time it could have been thought that British justice had reached these heights, but evidence regarding police corruption and the concealing of evidence does little to help the retribution argument.

Another argument against the death penalty is that it removes any hope of reforming or reclaiming the criminal for society. This argument figures in the Christian perspective, which stresses moral restoration. Yet, as we have seen, there is no guarantee that a released criminal will not kill again or that he will show repentance for what he has done. Perhaps this is because our prisons are designed not to change people but to discipline and punish them. On the other hand, the prospect of the death penalty not only, as Dr Johnson said, concentrates the mind most wonderfully but also has been known to induce repentance for the deed done. Theologians who want to oppose the death penalty have to move away from the teaching of the Old Testament and have difficulty in finding an example of how Jesus might have thought on this matter.

Forgiveness and love do figure prominently in his teaching, but the Sermon on the Mount appears to be dealing with personal relationships and does not give guidance on how a state should act when it is seeking to uphold its laws. But there is a particular passage which, while not appearing in the best manuscripts of the New Testament, does show how Jesus handled a case of adultery. The story is in the spirit of Jesus and would appear to have an important bearing on our discussion. The scribes and Phari-sees brought a woman caught in adultery to Jesus and pointed out that the Jewish Law demanded that she receive the death penalty. Jesus stooped and wrote on the ground. What did he write? This has caused much speculation and one of the best theories is that he wrote the sins of the accusers on the ground! This agrees with Jesus' statement, 'Let him who is without sin among you be the first to throw a stone at her' (John 8:7). Now those who oppose the death penalty from a Christian point of view point to the treatment of the woman and say that Jesus raises the issue of the moral authority of judge and executioner and asserts his right to forgive her sin. Without doubt these judges were not in a position to judge because they had either committed the same sin without being caught or were sinners in a general sense. But Jesus did not think the sin was of no account and warned her not to commit it again.

However, it is difficult to apply this story to a different crime, such as murder. First, in the case of adultery we are thinking on a sexual basis, and few could claim that thoughts of such a sin had not entered into their minds, even if they had not committed the act. Hence we need to be careful in judging others. Second, our modern laws would view adultery in a much less severe way than first-degree murder. Again, a modern jury would be selected in such a way as to prevent anyone guilty of a crime from sitting on it, so that they could not be accused of judging another when they had committed a similar act. The story is in the spirit of Jesus, as we have said. He generally kept the laws of the Jews but broke them when the needs of humanity demanded it, as in his dealings with Sabbath keeping. He may have seen in this case of adultery some extenuating circumstances, and he realised that the Jews were simply using the woman to try and catch him out. He did not condone the sin but let her off with the warning, 'Go and sin no more' (John 8:11).

RETRIBUTION

We have noted that arguments for the death penalty can be made on a Kantian basis or on a utilitarian one. The latter operates with the idea that the death penalty may deter others from committing the same crime, but we have noted that research is inconclusive on this matter. We might ask: Do numbers really matter? Could it not be argued that the majority of decent people are appalled by a brutal murder and that the death penalty relieves this distress? But, as Tom Sorell points out, the burden of proof would still be on those who favour the death penalty to demonstrate that it 'was not itself too awful a means of relieving legitimate distress. [Their argument] would have to show, for example, that public disquiet at violent crime was severe enough to justify the irreversible penalty of death rather than life imprisonment. It would have to show, again, that the reasons against killing in general were not strong enough to prohibit the relief of public distress by killing.'[10] Hence the need to consider the retribution argument.

Let us try and picture a society in which such retribution might work. Laws are imposed on the members of such a society with their consent, on the basis of freedom and equality. Each person recognises that he is free but that his freedom is limited by the freedom of others. Hence laws are created to provide balance and harmony and for the mutual protection of the members.

Everyone has the vote and the democratic representatives create the laws, which are based on justice for all. Now when someone commits a crime the state has the right to inflict punishment so that the balance due to everyman may be maintained. This means that the punishment must fit the crime, so that the person who has not respected either the property or the life of another must pay. The most precious possession that we have is life, and if someone takes it away from another he must forfeit his own life. In taking his life the state is not repeating the crime of murder but upholding the law, 'Thou shalt not kill'. How can the criminal atone for his crime except by his death? No amount of money can compensate the state for the breaking of its law or bring the victim back to life again or relieve the distress of his relatives.

Justice is based on the principle of equality. It cannot be prejudiced on one side or the other. It also needs to uphold the principle of equivalence between crime and punishment. The criminal knows that in breaking the law against killing he has brought the death penalty upon himself and has no right to complain. If we are to argue that death is too terrible a punishment for aggravated murder, then we must concede the principle of equality upon which justice is based, or else contend that the criminal is going to lose by the death penalty more than the victim lost in being murdered or that forgiveness and love are more important than justice.

If at this point someone contends from the Christian viewpoint that it is love and not justice that is important, then they will have to dispute the point made by Joseph Fletcher in the last chapter that justice is giving everyone his due. But according to Christianity the one thing due to everyone is love; hence love and justice are the same. However, it may be further argued that only God has the right to take life, since he gave it; in that case the criminal has disobeyed God in taking life. Moreover, according to the apostle Paul, the state is 'the servant of God', and its function is 'to vent wrath and vengeance on the man who does evil' (Romans 13:4). Paul's view was that whether a state knew it or not, it was doing God's work. If he could say this about Roman justice, which often went against the Christian, he could surely say it about the democratic state that we have pictured.

Finally, it could be argued that the victim suffers a greater evil than the murderer. As Tom Sorell points out, the victim 'not only has his life taken away but has it taken arbitrarily, without being guilty of wrongdoing, and in the absence of the safeguards of due process often extended to the criminal'.[11]

CONCLUSION

It would appear then, having made some attempt to assess the various arguments for and against the death penalty, that the retributive ground for it remains the strongest. This would be in the case of aggravated murder only. The execution of convicted terrorists would have the grave side-effect of creating martyrs and motivating others to follow the same path.

Deciding what crimes should earn the death penalty is a major problem, as Tom Sorell points out. He quotes Justice John Marshall Harlan: 'To identify before the fact those characteristics of criminal homicides and their perpetrators which call for the death penalty, and to express these characteristics in language which can be fairly understood and applied by the sentencing authority appear to be tasks which are beyond present human ability.'[12]

Those opposed to capital punishment will strongly agree with this statement but those for it, while acknowledging the problem, will still contend that their moral argument is strong enough to justify the undertaking of this highly difficult legal task.

Questions for discussion

- When do you think a utilitarian would allow punishment? Does he/she believe in deterrence or retribution? And why?
- If we are determined by nature and nurture how can we be responsible for crimes committed?
- Do you think that punishment should be proportional to the crime? If so, should capital punishment not be introduced?
- Suppose that 99 per cent of a population wanted to execute a convicted murderer, would a Kantian theory regard this as a strong reason for executing the convicted murderer? Would a utilitarian theory? Which is the more satisfactory approach?
- Is the death penalty 'a cruel and unusual punishment'?

FIVE

War

'It's murder, that's what it is!' cried a mother whose son had been killed in South Vietnam. 'What good comes of it?' she asked. This sense of futility was often conveyed to me by the Vietnam veterans whom I met in the USA both during and after the war. Their disillusionment sprang not only from the loss of young lives but also from the fact that the USA was allied with a corrupt regime in Vietnam, from the questions raised by the actions of American troops, from a feeling that America's part in the war was another example of imperialism, and from the realisation that the conflict was being conducted under the shadow of nuclear annihilation. Yet conscientious objectors to war are accused of lack of patriotism and courage and are made the butt of jokes. For most of us, brought up on a diet of TV films extolling the bravery and virtues of the servicemen who fought against Hitler, pacifism is a strange position, and we are likely to misunderstand it. Hence we shall look at it first of all and then go on to consider wars that are held to be just and holy.

PACIFISM

War has always been with us but it has often been questioned. Hinduism, one of the oldest religions, gives us in
the Bhagavad Gita a picture of the hero Arjuna questioning
his task of going into battle against his relatives. He considers that it would be better for him to die rather than kill
them, but he is told that death, which relates only to the
physical, does not harm the soul and that it is his duty as
a warrior to fight. The argument would seem to justify
killing and is a dangerous one. Yet the picture can be
interpreted in a spiritual sense. Gandhi, the lover of non-
violence, did this, seeing Arjuna's battle as the spiritual
war in which a man must fight against his temptations.
Buddhism, however, which emerged out of Hinduism, laid
down that killing was wrong and inculcated a compassion
for all living things. The Buddhist was not to participate in
revolts, rebellion or uprisings and it was a sin for him even
to watch a battle. One of the most striking converts to
Buddhism was the Maurya emperor Asoka (c. 270–232 BC)
who, as a result of his belief, turned from aggression to
peace. He also worked for social justice, set up hospitals
and a welfare programme and promoted religious tolerance.
However, a military strain of Buddhism also arose, and
Buddhists were involved in wars in China, Ceylon and
Japan. A kind of utilitarian justification was used for this.
The argument was that it was necessary to kill some in
order that many might be saved. Also, since the Buddha
did not believe in the concept of a soul, there was really
nothing to kill! In any case, it was better to kill someone
than to allow him to kill.[1]

In the case of Judaism there is a strong warlike element
in the tradition. God is spoken of as a warrior who delivers
his people from Egypt and who destroys the enemies of

Israel. But there is also the other strain which the pacifist emphasises that God should be relied on rather than force and which advocates compassion rather than violence (Isaiah 52:13 – 53:12). Defensive war is obligatory but optional wars for the extension of territory are not so justifiable. All wars are to be conducted with mercy towards non-combatants and without needless destruction. War is only justified if there is a constructive end.[2] The pacifist interpretation, however, fails to note the commands to destroy utterly the enemy (Exodus 23:23–24; Deuteronomy 7:1–2; Joshua 6:21).

Christianity in its beginning was pacifist, but it did not mean passivity. Jesus is portrayed in the Gospels not as the victim of circumstances but as the one who deliberately chose to go to Jerusalem in spite of warnings. Some see his activity in the Temple as revolutionary, but the view has not won acceptance. Neither has the view that his silence at his trial should be regarded as passive acceptance. He accepted suffering but resisted the ecclesiastical system of his day in word and deed, thus steering a middle course between revolution and passivity. He taught men and women to love their enemies, and since it was not in the Jewish dispensation to hate a personal enemy he must have meant the Romans.[3]

Paul followed this instruction and called on his converts to do good to the enemy (Romans 12:20–21). The claim that Christians were pacifists during the first 200 years is based on the views of the Fathers of the Church. Thus in the writings of Irenaeus, Clement of Alexandria, Tertullian, Origen and Cyprian we have statements which are summarised in Tertullian's terse phrase: 'Christ, in disarming Peter, ungirt every soldier.' But some people were converted while serving in the army, and Clement did not think that they should leave it. On the other hand, there is some evidence that serving soldiers could not become full Church members until they had left the army.[4] Tertullian records that they went to war with other soldiers and had difficulty when they were asked to participate in pagan religious ceremonies.

But it is argued that being a soldier was not really a major issue for the early Church, since few of its members were eligible for the army and they were more interested in the expected return of Christ than in military service. However, Christians did expect the state to keep order and to use discipline. They recognised, following the apostle Paul, that the civil powers 'bear not the sword in vain for the punishment of evildoers' (Romans 13:4). But there is evidence that in the third century individual Christians such as Maximilian, Tarachus and Marcellus were put on trial because they wanted to leave the army and would not fight. In the fourth century there is the case of Martin.

In general we may conclude that while Christianity remained a minority religion the issue of military service was not very important. But when, after the conversion of Constantine, the Roman Emperor, Christianity became the religion of the majority, there arose the need to establish the Christian attitude to participation in war.

THE JUST WAR

In the changed circumstances Augustine (354–430), following Cicero and Ambrose, developed the concept of the just war. He pointed out that Jesus ordered tribute money to be paid to Caesar and that this money was used to pay soldiers. He argued that the command 'resist not evil' meant an inward disposition, not a bodily action. According to Augustine, we must have love towards our enemies but, just as a loving father disciplines his son, so we must sometimes carry out warlike actions against our foes for their own good. Soldiers who came to Jesus were often commended for their faith and it is not recorded that he told them to give up their profession. While the Christian is against war in general he realises that at times wars must be fought in order to secure justice and peace.

Taking up the concept of punishment, Augustine maintains that the Old Testament teaches that God initiates wars to punish nations and uses the power of a state as an instrument to do this. But there is a tension in Augustine's teaching between his idea that killing is not allowed, which extends even to not defending yourself, and his idea that killing in war is acceptable. He argues that it is necessary for the soldier to obey the state and kill, for he must act as an obedient servant. This is a dangerous doctrine, since in modern times soldiers have tried to excuse dreadful acts on the grounds that they were acting under orders from their superiors.

Thomas Aquinas in the Middle Ages based his view on the teaching of Augustine. Any war must have the authority of the central ruler, its cause must be just and it must seek to realise a good end. Aquinas argued that Augustine was right in seeing the New Testament injunction not to resist evil as inward. With regard to the statement that those who take the sword shall perish by the sword, he contended that this did not apply to those in authority.

New criteria were added to the theory of the just war in the sixteenth century: the war must be fought by proper means; action should be against the guilty only; the innocent should not suffer; war must be undertaken as a last resort; and there must be a reasonable chance of success. Such a doctrine was of considerable comfort to rulers, for it stressed obedience to them. It also enabled them to declare that their going to war was just or as it has been put, 'self-vindication without the due process of law'. But some of the clauses of the just war theory have been useful, especially the thought of not going to war unless everything else has been tried and the stress on not injuring non-combatants. The last world war obviously infringed this. Thus during the bombing of German cities the issue was debated in the House of Lords. Bishop George Bell opposed such bombing despite the public feeling that tit for tat should be meted out to the Germans.[5]

In the past some pacifist groups felt that since the world had rejected the teachings of Jesus they ought to withdraw from politics, but this was not true of the influential Quakers. George Fox refused to fight for Cromwell, and William Penn went unarmed to sign a treaty with the Indians. One Quaker even undertook a mission to the Czar of Russia to inform him that war was wrong. The Friends Ambulance Unit has distinguished itself in the wars of the twentieth century.

There has been a variety of peace movements, both Christian and Humanist, advocating pacifism of one kind or another. Groups such as the Fellowship of Reconciliation, the Peace Pledge Union and the Campaign for Nuclear Disarmament, and individuals such as Bertrand Russell, J. B. Priestley, Victor Gollancz, Kingsley Martin and Canon Collins have had a decisive effect on our thinking about war today. In particular, they have influenced the Labour Party's policies on nuclear weapons.

But the greatest exponents of active non-violent resistance have been Mahatma Gandhi in India and Martin Luther King Jnr in America. Gandhi, influenced by his beloved Gita and the Sermon on the Mount, believed that to recognise evil and not to oppose it was to deny one's humanity. To recognise evil and to oppose it with the weapons of the evil-doer was to affirm one's humanity, but to recognise evil and to oppose it with the weapons of God was to affirm one's divinity.[6]

Both Gandhi and King, by the careful planning and execution of their opposition to injustice, showed that pacifism was no mere idealism. Protests, strikes and boycotts, resulting in imprisonment, beatings or even death, were carried through and had the maximum effect on world opinion. Discipline and reasonableness faced hatred and violence and won. Gandhi taught that it was permissible to defend oneself when attacked and in time of war to enlist as a medical orderly. If the war was just, it was possible to serve as a non-combatant.

Both King and Gandhi embraced the idea of pacifism as love which simply submits to an aggressor. They refused to cooperate with an unjust system and placed difficulties and inconveniences in its way. This was non-violent resistance. But it is argued that with a ruthless oppressor they would have been simply exterminated. The counter-argument is that 'the blood of the martyrs is the seed of the Church'. This is demonstrated by the fact that although many of the early Christians were thrown to the lions or set alight in Nero's gardens to entertain the crowds, their cause survived. Others argue that personal pacifism is all right as long as pacifists don't try to influence others, but national pacifism is impossible. However, some countries that say they are enlightened have imprisoned people for their personal pacifism. Among them have been some prominent philosophers such as Bertrand Russell.

But it would appear that the majority of people both here and in the USA would embrace some form of the just war theory rather than pacifism. We now need to ask how relevant the theory is with the advent of nuclear weapons.

As we have seen, the just war idea tries to indicate when one state may go to war with another and how the war should be conducted. One reason for such a war would be a just cause. In 1939 Britain, in going to war with Germany, was thinking of defending the rights of those countries that Germany had invaded, and the nation was fully behind this decision. It was taken with reluctance and only after an attempt at negotiation. When this failed the war was undertaken as a last resort. Now, in the context of nuclear weapons, some advocates of the theory would confine the undertaking of the just war to national defence. Nevertheless, the Gulf War was justified on the just war criteria.

The question of whether only a proper ruler or government can decide to go to war is more pertinent to the issue of revolution within a state and will be discussed in our next section.

What then of the rule which stipulates that non-combatants must not be harmed? The last world war breached this rule, since civilians were killed in the bomb attacks on Germany. However, there is debate about how innocent these people were, since vast numbers of Germans had fully supported Hitler.

HOLY WAR

Augustine had envisaged God conducting a war, so it comes as no surprise to us that successive popes decreed that killing infidels was acceptable. Pope Urban II (1088–1099) launched the First Crusade against Islam. Such a war, he thought, would recover the holy places for Christianity and would heal the breach between the Eastern Church and the Western. The amazing enthusiasm which this call to arms excited shows us the power of religion in those days. Not only soldiers but also peasants, artisans, the poor and the needy heard the battle cry and responded to it. They set out across Europe, passed through Asia Minor and Syria and entered Palestine. Stanley Windass writes: 'In any village street men could be seen loading their trivial belongings on to carts, hitching these to their oxen, and lumbering off with their wives and families to the Land of Promise. The children, soon weary of the journey, and doomed never to return, asked anxiously, whenever they saw a strange castle or town, "Is that Jerusalem?" '[7]

Jerusalem was to be their new home, where they would await the second coming of Christ and the arrival of his kingdom. The fact that this establishment of his kingdom by force was anathema to him did not seem to enter their heads. This shows how far they had moved from the Gospels.

Christianity was now involved in a bloody conflict with another religion which believed in the same kind of holy war. Islam, founded by the prophet Muhammad (born in AD 570), had swept into Sicily and Spain and had entered France but had been defeated at Poitiers in 732. The Crusades contributed to a long enmity between the two faiths. The *jihad* ('holy war') was considered just and was directed against the infidel. Ironically, Christianity was undertaking the Crusades for the same reason, despite the protests of its pacifists. But the pacifist trend is also found in Islam, particularly among the mystical Sufis, who generally have thought in terms of a spiritual war rather than a physical one.

Pacifism persisted both in Christianity and Humanism. There were the Waldenses, the Cathari, the Hussites, and Humanist scholars such as Erasmus. During the sixteenth-century Reformation there sprang up the Anabaptists and the Brethren, and somewhat later came the Quakers. The main Protestant Reformers, Calvin and Luther, believed not only in a just war but also in a holy one, and this contributed to the wars of religion in England with

Cromwell playing a leading part. It was usual for him and his troops to go into battle with the cry of the holy war on their lips: 'Let God arise and let his enemies be scattered!' (Psalm 68:1).

In the two world wars of the twentieth century the holy war concept was still in evidence. English Protestants in the First World War accused the Pope of being in favour of or even in league with the Austro-Hungarian Empire, and Catholic Belgium saw itself as a victim of the Teutonic fury of Protestant Germany. The Moslem Ottoman Empire thought of its war against the Christian powers of Britain, Russia and France as a *jihad*. In the Second World War German propaganda attempted to represent the war on the Eastern Front as a crusade by civilised Christendom against the atheistic forces of communism.

In general, as Francis Clark points out, there was a conviction among the Christians of the West and among world Jewry that in fighting the Nazis they were opposing an evil force which was the enemy of their beliefs.[8] Hitler was, on the other hand, in some ways presenting himself as a new messiah, leading his forces against the evils of communism, imperialism and Judaism. Thus both sides called upon God to help them in their wars.

In August 1990 the Iraqi president, Saddam Hussein, continued the holy war tradition and challenged the Arab world to wage a *jihad* against the Americans. He claimed, quite wrongly, that they and other infidels were occupying Islam's holy shrines in Saudi Arabia, when the truth was that they were there to protect the country from his aggression. Religion can often be used even today by dictators who want to whip up hatred to support their military ambitions.

THE NO-WINNER WAR

The advent of the atomic bomb has raised new and un-expected questions about the conduct of a future war. And yet it took a long time for the East and West to reduce their enormous arsenals. We want in this section to consider the pacifist's objections first of all and then to ask whether the just war theory is made irrelevant by the advent of nuclear weapons.

The pacifists mount the following case. The possession of nuclear weapons is dangerous, for an accident could happen that would spark off a retaliatory strike by the other superpower, and this would easily escalate into a nuclear holocaust. One cannot wait until the outbreak of such a war to express dissent; campaigns of civil dis-obedience must be carried out. Protests such as those at Greenham and Molesworth, the hindering of a Cruise Missile convoy exercise, a refusal to pay the proportion of one's tax which is used for military or nuclear purposes and mass demonstrations brought the pacifist's case before the public in a way that words cannot.

Intentions can be good or evil. While a person cannot be punished for intending to kill, the longer he harbours the thought, the more likely he is to commit the deed. To give up the evil intention of using nuclear weapons is to be morally improved. A reply to the pacifist might be that we do not intend to use the weapons – we are only bluffing but, the pacifist will say, if we are bluffing we will need to keep this a secret not only from the enemy but also from our own people. It would be difficult to do this. Also, it would be hard to base a strategic policy on a bluff. Circumstances could arise which would force a country to abandon the bluff and carry through the threat. These circumstances could be used as a justification for employing the weapons, for the consequences of not using them would be judged worse than those of using them.

The pacifist case implies that it would be better to be 'red' than 'dead'. To the patriot and warlike nations this is impossible. But the pacifist develops this case by pointing out that Russia, for so long regarded as the enemy, now appears to have a more human face. Even if we had to submit to Soviet control we could lend our weight to the bringing of more democracy into the system. Bertrand Russell argued that Soviet domination could be mellowed and that, in any case, freedom is limited even in democratic countries.

Before *glasnost* the choice, according to the pacifist, was really between Soviet domination and a holocaust. The arms race made such a disaster more likely. Despite the enormous cost, the two superpowers had developed the hydrogen bomb, ballistic missiles and the submarine-launched Polaris. In the USA at the height of the arms race almost 90 per cent of public monies for research was being spent on 'defence'. Scientists such as Oppenheimer who opposed the developments were banished from the system. Spending on this vast scale could not be continued, particularly when it might be spent on relieving the awful distress of Third World countries.

Having considered some of the pacifist's arguments, which would lead to a plea for disarmament, we now look at those of their opponents, who contend that the building up of such weapons is necessary for the purpose of deterrence.

The pacifist's case is idealistic. We know that we need to use force in a world such as ours: a criminal must be prevented from killing his victim; a woman must resist a rapist; we must deter other nations from attacking us. Even if the West had to submit to the East (and such submission is not in the tradition of the USA or Britain), there would be no guarantee that China, which possesses nuclear weapons, would not engage in a war with Russia which would destroy humankind. But the West has no intention of using its weapons in a first strike against any enemy. They are there to maintain the balance of power.

It is also possible to have a limited nuclear war with some degree of success against an opponent. The 'Star Wars' programme was intended to develop some kind of umbrella screen against a strike by the opponent. The pacifist sees submission to the enemy as the first stage in his policy, but would engage in protests about lack of freedom and mount campaigns of disobedience which would make the running of the conquered state impossible. The non-pacifist contends that this policy would result in more deaths and suffering than would engaging the enemy in war. A utilitarian would try to calculate the foreseen effects of each policy, presuming that a limited nuclear war could take place. However, it is difficult to make such calculations.[9]

The pacifist insists that the cost of stockpiling nuclear weapons is enormous. But the weapons industry was a major factor in the post-war economic boom. Government funding of the scientific-military-industrial complex created substantial employment for the labour force in America. Only international competition and the development of the European Economic Community and Japan halted the boom in the USA. Since the later 1960s she has been forced to reduce her arms spending, although it still remains high. However, the arms industry has found new markets for conventional weapons in countries torn by civil war. The Gulf War revealed that both East and West had supplied Iraq with arms.

Opponents of pacifism argue that disarmament would be

a major disaster for the US economy, since strategic arms development stimulates a capitalist goods sector in a way that spending on peaceful programmes such as public welfare would not do.[10] Some opponents of pacifism also invoke the just war theory. The cause is just, for if Russia attacked we would reply by way of self-defence. We have given an assurance to them that we will not strike first. It is possible to conduct a limited nuclear war and there is some hope of success. Further, military and not civilian targets would be aimed at.

We now turn to a consideration of the arguments which we have looked at in this chapter, and we start with the point that the just war theory does not seem to apply in this age of nuclear arms. It is impossible to say with certainty that a limited nuclear war will not escalate into a total one and it is difficult to predict success. It is estimated that the dropping of the first two atomic bombs on Japan killed 200,000 people, and civilian dead were recorded as upwards of 180,000. No one can adequately describe the appalling horror of this or accurately predict what would happen if weapons of greater power were to be used. It is reckoned by conservative estimates that in an all-out war with Russia there would be 20 million dead in the USA – and this would be a limited war that would stop short of a holocaust. The price of success is too high.

It is claimed that the victims of the bombings of Hiroshima and Nagasaki suffered from radiation sickness and that their children experienced radiation-induced disorders. This was the result of only two simple bombs. But now the arms race has produced much more devastating bombs and ballistics; the effect of their use is unthinkable. One cannot be certain that it would be possible to control such a war if it ever broke out, since there is doubt that the opposing sides would be able to maintain communication with one another. The most likely outcome would be a nuclear winter from which the survivors would be unlikely to recover.

Currently we do not believe that Russia has any intention of attacking the West, so there is no need to have such weapons to deter her. Economically, she is moving away from a communistic policy to one that to some extent resembles the capitalist system. There are those, of course, who argue that we must continue to build up a weapons arsenal, because new opponents arise and there are large numbers of people involved in the arms industry. Scaling down that industry would mean much unemployment. But it has been shown that dictators can be dealt with without nuclear weapons. Also, there are ways of providing employment for people other than the arms industry. The main aim should be to prevent the proliferation of nuclear weapons.

Today the pacifists' arguments are gaining strength. Various policies are put forward. Some advocate all dismantling of nuclear weapons, and some say that they should be 'frozen' by multilateral accord and then gradually reduced. Then there is the unilateralist approach, which argues that we should scale down our weapons, even if Russia does not reciprocate. Such a gesture of good will was embraced by the Church of England's General Synod in its report *The Church and the Bomb* (1982).

What is significant is that the Russians took the initiative, calling for a reduction of the nuclear stockpiles and actually discarded some of their own weapons, when it should (arguably) have been the West which undertook the steps of reconciliation. Indeed, when the history of the Cold War is looked at, there is evidence that the West is partly to blame for the atmosphere of distrust and suspicion that built up between the Allies during the Second World War. Britain and the USA were suspicious of communist ideology with its gospel of world revolution, and thus the development of the atomic bomb was kept secret from the Russians.

It is strongly argued that the atomic bomb was used against Japan in order to save American lives and end the war quickly, but some contend that the bombing was also intended to intimidate Russia and to prevent the need for her to invade Japan. It could also have been done to justify the tremendous cost to the American taxpayer which was involved in the bomb's development.

The suspicion which built up during the post-war years has not been easy to overcome. It must be granted that pacifism in its various forms has tried to do this with its movements and campaigns for peace, its international workshops, its call for the inclusion of peace studies in the curricula of schools and its non-violent action.

Since the breaking down of the Berlin Wall and the disintegration of the Soviet Union in 1991 religious freedom became a reality. Previously Russian Orthodox churches had been closed, bishops imprisoned and religious minorities persecuted. It was estimated that 200,000 priests were killed during Communist rule. Only in the 1980s did the assault on Orthodoxy diminish and other religions allowed to develop with the *peristroika* of Mikhail Gorbachev. The Russian Orthodox Church has been accused of passivity during the time of persecution but it is an example of non-violence and martyrdom which aided its survival and increased its moral influence.

While wars continue in various countries the main threat remains in nuclear weapons which have proliferated so that an estimated fifteen countries other than the superpowers now possess them.

REVOLUTION

In the post-war period there have been many revolutions, especially in Third World countries. Revolutionaries aim at the overthrow of the existing political and social order and its power structure, which they consider oppressive, unjust and based on inequality and discrimination.

All in some way show the influence of Karl Marx (1818–1883), who concentrated on the unholy trinity of economics – that is, property, labour and class. War, said Marx, springs from capitalism, in which the middle class or bourgeoisie dominates the working class or proletariat. The bourgeoisie will not give up their power without a struggle; hence violence is inevitable. The revolution, when it comes, aims at a classless society and a state which itself will 'wither away' and become the dictatorship of the proletariat. This rule of the people has not taken place, nor has there been a fulfilment of Marx's other prediction, namely that capitalism would be replaced by communism in Europe. The communist revolutionary leaders have formed dictatorships which have been just as oppressive as those which they overthrew. As evidence of this we have Stalin's reign of terror, condemned by the communists themselves, and the oppressive clampdown on student protest in China.

But the Third World countries, plagued by poverty and injustice, have experienced capitalist exploitation over the years and see the Marxist analysis of the situation as very accurate. They confront us today with the challenge: 'We are poor because you are rich.' The only solution, as they see it, is the Marxist concept of a complete transformation of society. No mere reform of society is sufficient.

The conditions are right. In many countries there is a mood of expectation among the masses. They are determined to get political rights and better working conditions and wages. In such situations charismatic leaders have arisen who kindle the imagination and energy of the people and ignite their hopes and dreams. Castro in Cuba, Mandela in South Africa, Martin Luther King Jnr in America ... Some have been violent, others non-violent, but they have all had the same magnetic appeal for the people, who have been willing to follow them to the death.

However, revolutions can fail to deliver freedom, and they can cost too many lives. The cost of failure must be weighed carefully, and what comes after the revolution, if it happens to be successful, needs to be carefully planned.

Gandhi and King took up their cause with an emphasis on non-violent active resistance. Others invoked the just war criteria. In South Africa the revolutionary movement, the African National Congress, initially tried to bring about change by non-violent means, but after the massacre at Sharpville, when 69 blacks were killed and 180 were injured, they turned to the armed struggle. In 1964 Nelson Mandela and other leaders of the revolution were sentenced to life imprisonment and it was only after years of protest that they were released. He subsequently became prime minister of the country and his successor has promised to continue the reforms. But some argue that fear and violence are continuing and it is difficult to view the prospects optimistically. While Mandela denied that he was a communist, the ANC charter stresses the rule of the people, the redistribution of wealth, the sharing of the land, equality before the law, nationalisation, free education and so on.[11]

Africa has been a seed-bed of revolution ever since the end of the colonial period. It is estimated that 15 countries have had one coup since independence and that 15 others have had two or more. By 1983 50 governments had been overthrown in independent Africa and 30 countries had experienced a coup. The reasons for this instability are tribal diversity and enmity, shaky economics and competing land claims. Dissidents have been killed, detained or exiled in a South African manner as the parliamentary democracy imposed by the colonial powers has broken down and the dictators have emerged.

But the place where revolutions seem to occur with greatest frequency is South America, though many of them have not been successful. It would be better to term them uprisings rather than revolutions. After Castro's victory in Cuba in 1959 it was thought that the continent would explode in revolution, but the only Marxist to achieve power after Castro's victory was Salvadore Allende, who became President of Chile in 1970.

A look at Castro's revolution shows that many of the conditions for successful revolution were present, especially a shaky economy. It is economics which makes politics and not vice versa. In spite of American investment, incomes were little higher in the 1950s than they had been in the 1920s, and this affected the middle class as well as the working class. There was a great deal of student political activity, as many graduates were unemployed or underemployed. Castro himself was a student at the University of Havana.[12]

Batista's government was weakened by the corruption and jealousy of senior officers in the army, and Castro had the support of the people. Strikes, demonstrations, sabotage and propaganda aided the guerrillas, and the brutality of the police and the army lost Batista his remaining popular support.[13] What of the goal of the revolution? Here judgement is mixed. On the one hand, Castro's regime was authoritarian. At the end of the 1960s he admitted that there were some 20,000 political prisoners in Cuba, and by late 1968 about 350,000 Cubans had gone into exile – nearly 5 per cent of the population. But on the other hand, conditions for the poor improved with free education, free clothing for children, free medical care for all, cheap (albeit rationed) food and apparently full employment. This was a considerable advance compared with pre-Castro regimes.[14]

It is the goal of a revolution which those in opposition to it fear, for they do not know what their position will be and whether justice will emerge for minorities as well as for the majority. The history of revolution shows that the oppressed of today can become the oppressors of tomorrow.

Power corrupts. Often much thought is given to the careful planning of the revolution but not to how the various leaders and groups who will jostle for power afterwards are to be handled. Consequently an authoritarian regime often emerges.

The place of religion both as an obstacle to revolution and as a possible assistance to it can now be examined. Marx viewed religion in nineteenth-century England as supporting the status quo by endorsing the idea that God had ordered the class system. We hear this in the children's hymn:

> The rich man in his castle,
> The poor man at his gate;
> God made them high and lowly
> And ordered their estate.

Religion was 'the opium of the people' but it was also 'the cry of the oppressed'. Unfortunately this cry was not strong enough to bring about a fundamental change in the social order. What people needed, said Marx, was a change in social and working conditions; religion was too busy saving the soul and pointing to a heaven where wrongs would be righted. In all fairness it must be said that Christianity did produce social reformers, but Marx would have seen them as middle-class people dispensing their bounty to the poor. Instead, thought Marx, the poor themselves must rise and by revolution destroy the system. Only when the workers had overthrown the middle class, abolished private property and taken the means of production into their own hands would there be a chance of establishing the kingdom of humanity upon the earth.

Revolution is not simply a matter of removing a tyrant but also entails liberating the people, who are to rule when the power of the state which they have created has 'withered away'. One defect is that so far the state has not withered away as Marx thought it would. Further, Marx expected revolutions to occur in the industrialised states, but in fact they have usually happened in countries with rural and peasant populations, such as China and Russia. Indeed, Marx has had a greater influence on thinking in the Third World. Ironically, in that context religion is sometimes seen as backing revolution.

Marx was the descendant of a long line of Jewish rabbis, and in his denunciation of the oppression of the poor he dons the mantle of the Hebrew prophet. Justice, equality and freedom are major Old Testament themes. The prophets thundered against a religion which thought more of temple worship than of the workers' conditions and whose members deprived the poor when they got the chance. Christianity too, in its beginnings, had strong socialistic and communistic overtones. There is a revolutionary sound about the Magnificat: 'He has put down the mighty from their seats and has exalted the humble and the meek. He has filled the hungry with good things and the rich he has sent empty away' (Luke 1:52–53). The early Church had a dramatic social impact: 'These that have turned the world upside down are come here also' (Acts 17:6). Again, the Marxist slogan, 'To each according to his need, from each according to his ability', would apply very neatly to the sharing and structure of the early Church: 'All that believed were together and had all things common; and they sold their possessions and goods and parted them to all, according as any had need' (Acts 2:44–45). A distribution of property that would please any communist!

Viewed in this way, Christianity could inspire and assist a revolution, and in South Africa and Latin America this has been the case. A theology emerged which saw God as the Liberator of the oppressed, leading his people out of bondage, just as he led the Israelites out of Egypt. The philosophers and theologians of the past have tried to interpret the meaning of suffering, but what is needed, as Marx said, is to change the world and remove the cause of the suffering. The fact is that we do not live in a rational world; you cannot negotiate with tyrants. Is it reasonable that the European Economic Community piles up 'mountains' of food and allows poverty to exist in Africa, Asia and Latin America? The Church talks about compassion and love of one's neighbour but supports governments which show a lack of concern for the poor.

How can so-called Christian nations engage in an arms race when millions are starving? Faced with such lack of understanding and care, the liberation theologians looked at the criteria for the just war, fastened on the 'last resort' clause and gave their support to revolution.

Basic restructuring of the Roman Catholic Church was needed so that it would become the church of the poor in Latin America. Communities were formed consisting of fifteen to twenty families. They began to meet weekly to read the Scripture and share their problems. Now there are upwards of 70,000 groups in Brazil. They are not separate from the Catholic Church but remain within it. The argument is that the middle class cannot build churches for the poor, since such churches would reflect the bourgeois structure of society. The corruption of power and class is present in the church, and it reflected the repression in society as a whole when it tried to silence the liberation theologians. The Franciscan priest Leonardo Boff was banned by the Catholic Church from publishing or teaching his views for a year. Boff sees the church as characterised by a form of religious monopoly capitalism. This means that the clergy control the theology, the sacraments and the administration. Hence a restructuring is needed 'from below' rather than 'from above'.[15]

Priests have been known to join guerrilla movements. A famous case was that of the Columbian priest Camil Torres who, appalled by the poverty of the people and accepting some of the Marxist analysis of the situation, formed the United Front of the Columbian People in 1965. He said: 'Love of neighbour has moved me to join the revolution. I shall not say Mass, but I will flesh out that love of neighbour in the temporal, economic and social sphere. When my neighbour has nothing to reproach me for, when the revolution has been carried through, then I will go back to saying Mass once again.'[16] On 15 February 1966 he was killed in an ambush by government troops. In Latin America he became a folk hero.

In South America and South Africa liberation theology produced a crop of detentions, bannings and deportations. As Caesar Aguiar wrote of the Latin American situation:

> The daily events in the life of the church go far beyond the expectation of the ordinary Christian. Five years ago, who would have thought in our continent priests would be murdered, Christians persecuted, priests deported, the catholic press silenced and attacked, ecclesiastical premises searched etc? Probably nobody.

Five years ago even the most radical Christians viewed events through utopian lenses and did not grasp their dramatic historical implications.[17]

Support for such a theology can be found in the Exodus from Egypt, in the just wars in the Old Testament, in the prophetic denunciation of the rich and of their oppression of the poor, in S. G. F. Brandon's thesis that Jesus was a Zealot with active Zealots among his twelve disciples, and in the communistic nature of the Early Church (Acts 2:44f). Further, it can be argued that the passivity of the early Church was due to a belief in the imminent return of Christ; hence their lack of revolutionary zeal is not binding on us.

But this theology does not fit easily into the pacifism of the early Church, and is more in accord with the just war theory. It wants to use the tools of Marx's social theory but rejects his view of religion – namely, that it is man-made and that once a just society has been reached it will disappear. It is difficult to see how Christian values are to be inculcated after a revolution which has been built on force. The early Church was composed mainly of the poor but it also included what we would call middle-class people. The early record shows that the community had people who owned property and were willing to sell it for the sake of the poor, although this was not required of them.

The account in Acts tells of freedom and equality, and it appears that there was a solidarity of those who had and those who had not. Poverty was not a virtue and money was not condemned, although love of it and refusal to share were. All of which shows that liberation theology is right, although it tends, like Marxism, to think of the working class as virtuous and of the middle class as villains. Marx did recognise that some of the middle class, with compassion towards the poor, would drop down into the proletariat and become leaders. Torres, who came from a middle-class background, did just this. The Church should be opposed to the rich–poor distinction, as the Epistle of James shows, but it is difficult to achieve a classless society. For example, in communist Russia privileges and power appear to be given to the leaders, administrators and executives, so that they look very much like a new upper class. The Church started as a small group in society, but as the institution grew and became the Church of the majority a bureaucracy developed, as happens in all organisations. It was necessary in order to preserve order and discipline. However, through this process the Church lost the flexibility, spontaneity, enthusiasm and charisma of its beginnings. Its structures became rigid and unjust and impeded good people from operating justly within it. Liberation theology's protest against this state of affairs is a good corrective, and the Catholic Church has taken note of this.

Revolutions which have resulted in communistic governments have brought about certain gains. Russia has progressed from being a country in a state of failure and disarray to being a superpower which rivals the USA. But economically she has not fared so well. A free market economy seems to be the only way forward, which is ironic: capitalism has returned to a country which thought it had abolished it for ever.

CONCLUSION

The causes of war – poverty, aggression, injustice and inequality – need removing, and various ideas and programmes have been put forward to do this. The ideals of pacifism, education, international programmes of friendship and reconciliation, the unification of religions, understanding between ideologies . . . all these can play a part. The negotiations between the superpowers and their signing of treaties are steps forward in the reduction of the nuclear threat. These developments have sent a sigh of relief around the world.

With regard to peacemaking, the United Nations has done better than the old League of Nations, perhaps because it has had a more universal membership. In addition to supplying peace-keeping forces to countries in a state of turmoil, it has specialised agencies which run educational programmes and work for international communication and co-operation. The United Nations has conducted wars in various places following the failure of all attempts to resolve the situation by other means. Iraq and Kosovo became household names as the struggle intensified to suppress dictators and restore human rights. But there is debate about the nature and extent of such involvement in the affairs of states. Some argue against it saying that the UN has got involved in local squabbles instead of concentrating on major issues. But surely the Gulf War and subsequent events were major problems, for, apart from a dictator encroaching on another's territory, it is essential that he does not get hold of nuclear weapons. We have a global responsibility for a just order in the world, so states exist for the common good, not simply to maintain justice in their own country. As long as the just war criteria are fulfilled intervention can take place. How can we stand aside and not notice appalling suffering in a particular country due to a tyrant? We can hardly subscribe to the view that military intervention is only possible to safeguard our national assets.[18]

While a new world order is a distant goal, and internal conflicts have multiplied, there is always the hope of a better understanding emerging between East and West. Russia requires aid from the West and needs to co-operate with America, but the repeat of the 1994–96 war against Chechnya had a bad effect on the relationship. Russia launched the assault as a reprisal for alleged bomb attacks in Moscow, but its ferocity and the desperate plight of the refugees seeking to escape from air strikes and without food, electricity or heating in sub-zero temperatures raised world-wide condemnation. And while the UN had intervened in other places there is little likelihood of military intervention against a superpower. In cases like these protests and diplomatic overtures are the only way, and this can foster solidarity and the idea of one world. As John Ferguson said, 'When men have set foot on the moon, it is ridiculous that we belong to quarrelling cliques.' Or, as John Donne aptly put it, 'No man is an island, entire of itself; every man is a piece of the Continent, a part of the main . . . any man's death diminishes me, because I am involved in Mankind.'[19]

A global approach to peace-making might be based on the following principles: respect for the territorial integrity of states, the inviolability of national borders, rejection of the use of force in mutual relations, limiting the arms race by undertaking not to increase existing stockpiles and a commitment to non-proliferation, acceptance of minimum levels of mutual tolerance in the political and cultural spheres, and willingness to jointly marshall resources and foster the development of the less affluent countries.

Without such principles, any new order that emerges will be written in sand.[20]

Questions for discussion
- How strong is the case for pacifism?
- Has modern warfare made the just war criteria obsolete?
- Is there any justification for engaging in a holy war?

- Liberation movements which involve violence have sometimes been inspired by religion. Is this possible?
- The United Nations should not intervene in the affairs of states. Do you agree?

SIX

The Moral Framework of Religions

In this chapter we consider in a limited way religions other than Christianity and their attitudes towards the issues which we have discussed. Religions operate in a framework of meaning based on the principle that members, except those of Theravada Buddhism, belong to God and have a duty to serve him and humanity. Such communities have an identity, common interests, moral obligations and may be legalistic or flexible regarding past traditions. All in theory are committed to brotherhood and sisterhood, love of the neighbour, justice, mercy and peace.

Laws of behaviour are based on the scripture, tradition and teaching of the religion but situations can arise that call for judgement to be based on compassion. Arguing from situations to principles or laws is called 'bottom-up', while the reverse is 'top-down'. The situational approach could lead to moral relativism but a line has to be drawn somewhere. Jesus, for example, in dealing with the woman taken in adultery was well aware of the Torah (Jewish law) but he went beyond it in his compassion and generosity. He knew what forced such women into prostitution and how they were used by men. He accepted the framework of the law but interpreted it in a flexible way. Nevertheless she was told not to break it in future: 'Go and sin no more' (John 8:11).

The Jews operate in a legal framework but the orthodox group are more strict about the laws than the progressives who stress individual decision. But both hold that there are absolute rules forbidding idol worship, adultery and the killing of the innocent. Jews do not accept original sin, that there is a causal connection between the sin of Adam and the subsequent sin of humanity (Psalm 51:5; Romans 5:12), but see the disobedience of Adam as a prototype not a burden of guilt transferred to his descendants. Everyman is 'the Adam of his own soul'. There is an evil inclination (*yetzer ha-ra*) in us but we can resist it.[1]

The Jewish legal system is called Halakhah which assists the individual in her decisions.[2] Free will is given a proper place and there is a going beyond law in forgiveness and generosity. If the Torah does not give guidance on a matter then authorities can be consulted or a court of law. There is also a place for natural law: a moral sense or conscience which enables us to behave in a moral way. But this is a subjective criteria of what is right or wrong: people of 'good conscience' have kept slaves. Some interpreted the natural as meaning the natural order of things which resulted in class systems.

As well as the Torah (the first five books of the Bible) there is the oral law enshrined in the Mishnah and the Talmud. The progressives hold that the Torah has a human input and has been edited by scholars over the years. They also consult rabbinic commentaries and philosophers when making decisions. Overall there is a basic principle: life is given by God and is sacred, so we ask about any action, Does it benefit humanity? In the case of cloning if it is done from personal vanity it is clearly wrong, but if beneficial then it may be acceptable.

Euthanasia on demand is not permitted but if the quality of life is poor and the condition terminal then it would be justified. The doctrine of double effect is acceptable. With regard to abortion the traditional Jewish teaching holds that the foetus has no status until birth: babies of thirty days who died were not given a full funeral. Abortion is not murder but serious, permitted only when the foetus is a threat to the sanity of the mother or her life, or the result of rape, or when the foetus is disabled. In the area of capital punishment the Jewish Sanhedrin followed the Old Testament teaching that there must be blood for blood and Israel has carried out executions for war crimes committed by the Nazis.[3]

Concerning war, the Jews have been in continual conflict with the Arabs regarding the land of Palestine and achieved such success in the Six Day War of 1967 and the Yom Kippur War of 1973 that many have seen the hand of God in it. Israel occupied Jerusalem, the West Bank, Judaea and Samaria. Zionism was delighted with these successes but the ultra-orthodox (haredim) were not pleased since they believe that the coming of the Messiah should set up the state of Israel. Only protracted negotiations witnessed in the latter half of the twentieth century resulted in the return of land to the Palestinians. The difficulty of judging when a defensive war becomes a war of aggression is posed and some Jews question if it is morally right to wage wars of conquest to strengthen their defence.

Islam bases its morality on the Qur'an, the sayings and example of the Prophet (*sunnah*), consensus of the people (*ijma*) and analogy (*giyas*). In this way the Muslim can follow the right path (*sharī'a*) and emulate the example of the Prophet who was the perfect man. The shariah (law) summarises the commandments which are interpreted by the various schools and expounded by the Mullahs and the

Ayatollah. The principle of analogy is used to extend the scope of the shariah so that when the Qur'an forbids anything, such as alcohol, it can be extended to drugs, tobacco and so on, but the law schools vary in their acceptance of this ruling.[4]

There are three basic groups in Islam: the Sunni, the Shi'ah and the Sufis. The Sunni make their decisions on a communal basis but the Shi'ah are inclined to accept the ruling of their leading scholars. With them the Iman is a scholar and advisor and there is immediate access to him on family matters. However, some of the younger Muslims want to find out for themselves and consult the Qur'an directly. The impact of modernity has meant a greater stress on individualism and relativism of values which causes problems for the consensus of the Sunni. While Islam insists that its laws are tempered with gentleness, humility and patience, some Muslims regard particular codes of the shariah as valid only in their context and hold to the underlying principles which supersede specific rulings in the Qur'an itself.[5]

Muslims have five pillars which are obligatory (*fard*). The first is the confession: 'There is no god but God, and Muhammad is his Messenger' (*shahadah*). The second is prayer or salat. The body must be clean, a certain posture is required, and it takes place at dawn, noon day, before sunset and sleep. The third pillar is fasting, or *saum*, and this occurs during the month of Ramadan and involves Muslims in the experience of the suffering of the less fortunate. The fourth pillar is charity, or *zakat*: the giving of a proportion of money to the poor. The last pillar is pilgrimage, or *Hajj*, to the holy city of Mecca. This is expensive and yet considered to be a duty for all. Those who are unable to meet the cost have sometimes tried to reach Mecca by foot which has meant devoting a

long time to it. There was also a sixth pillar, holy war
(*jihad*), but this is now rejected by many Muslims who
argue that it was added by one of their sects, the Khawarizi.
But it is a duty according to the Qur'an to fight for their
faith if differences cannot be resolved by peaceful means.
It is clear that force was used by Islam to conquer land but
not to make people Muslims. War is undertaken as a last
resort and the Islamic conflicts were part of the competing
for empire by several nations at that time.[6]

At least, this is the mainstream view but militancy has
erupted in modern times. Islamic groups were involved in
the killing of Anwar Sadat in 1981, and Hamas, the Arabic
Islamic Resistance Movement, demanded a jihad against
Israel. It opposed the Palestinian Liberation Organisation
led by Yasser Arafat because it was not strictly Muslim and
supported Ayatollah Khomeini in his Iranian revolution. In
Afghanistan the success of the Afghan Muslim (Mujhadin)
in 1992 created the fear that such militancy would spread
to other countries and it was confirmed by the repression
which followed under the Taliban. The militancy of Islam
also has its roots in the protest against the Western system
of taking interest on money loaned. Capitalism, it is
asserted, means that the rich get richer and the poor poorer.
The Shah of Iran, accused of destroying the Islamic state,
was deposed in 1979 and Khomeini bluntly embraced the
jihad proclaiming that people could only be made obedient
by the sword. But Iranians are Shi'ite, which is a minority
group in Islam, whereas the Sunni is mainstream and rejects
such violence. They would not accept the elevation of an
Imam such as Khomeini and a state ruled by religious
jurists.[7]

Turning to more everyday matters, the religion calls for
marital duties and the care of elderly parents. Recommended duties are hard work and the pursuit of knowledge

(*mandub*). Some behaviour is tolerated (*makruh*) while other is neutral (*mubah*). Muslims are also forbidden to drink alcohol, eat pork or gamble. Islam places stress on intention contending that an action is good only when it has a pious intent (*niyyah*). But despite a good intention, a bad action remains bad. The role of free will is a problem in Islam because there is a strong doctrine of predestination. Various answers have been proposed but none are satisfactory.[8]

Muslims believe in the equality of men and women but in practice the women have taken a secondary place. However, there are signs that this is undergoing change. Traditionally Islam insisted on severe penalities for murder, theft and adultery, but modern conditions require modification. In the case of adultery there must be no doubt in the mind of the judge and four witnesses are required who saw the act. A confession is needed which is difficult to obtain. It is emphasised that Allah is forgiving and merciful and should not be regarded as the God of vengeance.

The Qur'an states that to murder one person is to murder the whole of humanity, so the crime is grievous. Punishment is severe but usually commuted to prison or the payment of a fine. It is the deterrent aspect of punishment which is primary, but retribution is not forgotten. With regard to abortion life is sacred so the foetus has rights from the conception, but if the mother's life is in danger it has precedence over the foetus. Abortion is permitted if the mother feels that she cannot psychologically cope with the child, although abortion on demand is ruled out. There is the idea of the sleeping foetus which can be used to legitimise children born out of wedlock. After 120 days abortion is murder and accidentally induced miscarriage manslaughter. The foetus can inherit property. Some jurists justify abortion on economic grounds or possible deformity but such decisions are often left to the parents. Premarital sex is forbidden and rape is murder but contraception in marriage is acceptable.[9]

The moral framework of Hinduism is the acceptance of *dharma* which is a cosmic eternal principle. In practice it applies to performing duty according to class/caste. Thus the priest or brahman performs his duty by studying scripture (Veda) and leading the rituals which would not be appropriate for a person of lower caste. The latter is permitted to drink alcohol but it would be a sin for the brahman. One of the basic sources of morality is the Manusmrti, the law books, completed about the second century of the common era. They deal with marriage and the place of women who are generally called upon to be obedient to fathers and husbands. The Manu outlines the hierarchy of the social system: the brahmans or priests, the rulers, the commoners and the servants, and calls for the avoidance of wrong thinking which leads to action.[10]

Of course life in India is different from other countries and the migrant has to adapt as far as she can. In village Hinduism there is the belief that one God underlies everything despite the worship of demi-gods and the proliferation of images in temples. The Hindu forbids intoxication, gambling, illicit sex, and follows the path of unselfish action (karma yoga) which leads to a good rebirth. Many of them embrace the concept of bhakti which is love or devotion leading to the ardent worship of Vishnu whose incarnation, Krishna, appears in the Gita. Merit can be seen in Catholicism and Hinduism. The latter teaches that a life can be earned by previous actions (karma) and in the former saints can intercede because of their meritorious lives, and the sacrifice of Christ generated merit for all.

A radical trend is Tantrism which relativises the usually accepted values. It claimed that 'what is injurious becomes

spiritually useful and what is unethical becomes ethical'.[11]
The trend originated in asceticism which rejected the
normative Hindu dharma and went on to indulge in caste-
free sexual intercourse. Substances such as meat, fish and
alcohol were freely consumed and sex was seen as a way
to unity with the goddess Siva. Women are portrayed as
channels of power and knowledge and engage in what
orthodoxy would see as immoral practices. But it is argued
by some that sexual licence is exceptional and depends on
how radical the group is.

With respect to abortion many Hindus oppose it because
of the sanctity of life and the function of marriage as child-
bearing. Concerning suicide Ghandi said that it was not a
possibility because the spirit will weave for itself another
body.[12] Celibacy with him would appear to be better than
marriage because love can be extended to all instead of
being confined to the marital state. He opposed untouch-
ability as a cruel boycott of human beings. But despite his
stress on non-violence (*ahimsa*) he was assassinated in 1948
and his assassination was followed by the rise of
nationalism, a stress on Hindu identity, and conflict with
Islam. Right-wing movements such as the Bharatiya Janata
Party supported campaigns against the Muslims and dis-
puted the building of mosques. The mosque at Babri was
destroyed and thousands were injured in riots. In 1991
Prime Minister Rajiv Gandhi was assassinated. Resentment
against Muslims was high and the humanitarian work of
Mother Teresa was criticised because it was a foreign input.
This attitude and the use of force which is contrary to the
usual tolerance of Hinduism shows a warlike stance and
has induced fear in the hearts of Indian minorities.[13]

The Buddha taught that life is suffering due to desire
which must be eliminated and the way is the eightfold
path.[14] The first step is right viewpoint. If the perspective

is correct objects will not arouse desire for they will be seen as impermanent and insubstantial. There is no substantial 'self' (*anatta*): it is an illusion (*maya*). We are a collection of qualities and if there is no ego nothing can belong to it. Hence it is silly to say 'This is mine'. The ego continually desires power, money, wife, children and so on and these cravings lead to pain. The second step is the adoption of right values which do not relate to any ego. If I am always thinking of I, me, mine, it will result in false aspirations. These have to be replaced by love and kindness to all humanity.

The third and fourth steps are freedom from lying, slander, chatter and avoiding stealing. Any livelihood which involves the harming of other people such as the sale of intoxicating liquor or trafficking in women and slaves must be avoided. Hence right endeavour and right mindfulness and meditation on good things govern the actions of the will. Right contemplation rounds off this pathway.

There are strict rules for monks. They should be temperate in eating food, which is taken before noon, and not engage in or witness singing, dancing or the acting of plays. Garlands, perfumes, ornaments are forbidden and they must not rest on high or luxurious beds or accept gifts of gold or silver. In early Theravada Buddhism the right action was to abandon the world and cease to desire the objects of sense which only brought suffering. The best action for the lay person was to become a monk. The group of monks, the sangha, has a code with upwards of 227 offences and confession must be made even in connection with diet. Some offences result in permanent exclusion: killing a person, sexual intercourse, theft and falsely claiming higher knowledge.[15]

The Buddha pointed the way to liberation but each person must find his or her own enlightenment. No matter how depressed a person may be suicide is not the way out of the problems. Such a deed will by the law of karma mean a poorer existence in the next life. Only if the act has not the intention of getting a new body can it be blameless for then there will be no future effects. The Buddhist can point to monks like Channa and Vakkali and Godhika who committed suicide and were not condemned for they had no longing for a new life.[16]

These main types of Buddhism can be detected: Theravada, Mahayana, Vajrayana. Theravada has a spiritual élite (*nibbanic*) who within the monastic community pay attention to the intention of an action and aim at nirvana. The Buddha gave karma an ethical and psychological orientation focusing on intention. But the majority of Buddhists are on a lower spiritual dimension than the monks and have little understanding of karma. However, they seek to attain a good rebirth and possibly join the monks (*kammatic*) in another life. The main point is that morality relates to levels of spiritual attainment.

In Mahayana Buddhism the lay person has the opportunity of seeking nirvana, something which Theravada restricted to the monks. Help ethically is provided by the Boddhisattvas who delay their ultimate nirvana in order to help others. This tradition is more flexibile regarding the keeping of precepts: not telling the truth is possible in a difficult situation (skilful means). Thus a father may have to tell his child a lie to get them out of a burning house or in a country where only meat is eaten, a monk for whom this diet is forbidden, may eat it in order to win people to the Faith. Vajrayana goes further and encourages practices that violate the usual precepts. Killing is possible to prevent someone committing actions that would send him to hell, stealing to stop another stealing, adultery to provide better rebirths for the recently deceased etc.[17]

Buddhism follows its founder's teaching that all life is sacred but situations must be taken into account. Life-sustaining processes that merely prolong life are pointless. Let people die naturally in a peaceful atmosphere. Living wills are good, indicating wishes in advance. Passive eutha-nasia or letting die is embraced with the point that this is not a wish to end life but to end suffering. The basic intention is to relieve suffering not to kill. Active euthanasia of course is another matter and the Buddhist would oppose it and advocate the care of the hospice. The dangers of the elderly thinking that it was their duty to die rather than be a burden to their relatives is noted and must be avoided.[18]

With respect to abortion the foetus will be reborn and take on a new existence. Those who feel remorse for having an abortion can seek forgiveness through the various rituals and the helping of others. The foetus is a human being from conception, hence killing is only permitted if the life of the mother is in danger. The doctrine of double effect is acceptable. If the foetus is badly damaged there would be different attitudes to it. In most countries a woman, especially in the early stages of pregnancy, has the right to have an abortion or not. Buddhists accept contraception but under Chinese rule in Tibet they were forced to abort whether they wanted it or not. In general Buddhists say that abortion is like letting someone in by the front door and then throwing them out by the rear, so it is only acceptable under certain conditions.[19]

Since Buddhism is regarded as tolerant and accommo-dating it is surprising to discover militant groups. In Tibet there has been conflict between Buddhist groups and the Chinese. Some argue that the principle of compassion and the possibility of preventing greater suffering permitted forceful resistance to Chinese aggression. This is like the utilitarianism discussed in earlier chapters: the greater good overrules principles. But leaders have not been unanimous with regard to this. The thirteenth Dalai Lama advocated self-defence but the fourteenth Dalai Lama opposed it. In other parts of the world monks have immolated themselves and been involved in ethnic violence, for example Sri Lanka in the 1950s. The most religious group is the Janata Vimukti, or the National Liberation Front, which mounted an insurrection in 1971 and was not put down until 1990. The opponent was the Tamil Tigers, and Buddhists continue to refuse to make any concessions to them.[20]

The Sikhs believe in the brotherhood of humanity which includes both Hindu and Muslim. They repeat God's name (*nam japan*) daily not simply as a ritual but meditating on his attributes. Stress is put on earning an honest living (*karna*) and sharing hospitality with all (*vand chakhna*). Monastic life does not appeal, or celibacy. Like most religions they contribute money to the gurdwara (place of worship), oppose murder, adultery and resort to force only against evil. Love, hard work, dietary restrictions, service, tithing, marriage and family life are the values which they respect. There is a strict prescription against drugs, alcohol, tobacco and gambling, reflecting the influence of Islam. The five deadly sins are lust, anger, greed, worldy love and pride. But the Muslim emphasis on pilgrimage does not extend to Sikhism as their founder Guru Nanak did not favour it and other practices in Hinduism. Sikhs, however, do like to visit places associated with their founder Nanak and other Gurus and travel to Amritsar where their Golden Temple stands.

The community of the Khalsa was founded by Guru Gobind Singh in AD 1699. Men and women are admitted at an initiation ceremony involving the use of symbolic sugared water (*amrit*). The symbols of the Five K's are used to identify them: long hair to indicate saintliness, comb to remind of cleanliness, short sword showing the need to defend the weak, a steel bracelet worn on the wrist as a link to godly ideals, and shorts or trousers suitable for an active life.[21] Sikhism reacted against the caste system of Hinduism but in practice it still exists among them. The Sikhs are often regarded as warlike but they assert that they only turn to the sword as a last resort. They are called upon to 'kiss the feet' of their opponents but will not tolerate tyranny and oppression. Two of their Gurus were killed in non-violent protest.

However, the twentieth century has seen conflict between Sikhs and Hindus. Sant Jarnail Singh Bhindranwale who believed that many Sikhs were not living according to their traditions occupied the Golden Temple in Amritsar in 1984 and the Indian army launched an assault on the sacred place. He and his followers and many worshippers were killed. In turn the Sikhs assassinated Prime Minister Indira Gandhi, and violence has continued since that time with Sikh killing Sikh and Hindus taking revenge on them. The demands of the Sikhs are political, economic and religious. Most live in the Punjab which cuts them off from other Sikhs who dwell in Pakistan. Thus they are exposed to oppression from both Hindu and Muslim and feel very insecure. They demand a homeland (Khalistan) and many are prepared for martyrdom in order to achieve it. But some see Khalistan as a state of harmonious relationships between people rather than a particular place or political homeland. In 1995 the Chief Minister of Punjab, Beant Singh, was killed by Sikhs because they believed he had betrayed them. The world Sikh Sammelan convened in 1995 and tried to achieve a consensus but it did not enter into debate about Khalistan and some of the militant parties stayed away. Doubts remain if the militant tendency will ever disappear for the Jats, who are a large group, believe that war or the threat of it will attain their objectives.[22]

The Sikhs accept the just war concept tracing it back to Guru Gobind Singh who said: 'When all efforts to restore peace prove useless and no words avail, lawful is the flash of steel, it is right to draw the sword.'[23] The five conditions of the just war are similar to those we outlined previously but with certain modifications: there should be no enmity or desire for revenge, land should not be taken or property captured, nor should there be looting. Soldiers should not drink or molest the women and a minimum of force must be used.

Marriage is a sacred not a civil contract but divorce is allowed. There does not seem to be much opposition to contraception and abortion is permissible for the usual reasons, but termination must be done in the early stages. There is a debate among commentators on Sikhism regarding the discovery of the gender of the foetus. Some point out that Sikhs follow Hindus who outlaw the practice of scans and amniocentesis (birth test). But others disagree saying that the preference for boys has meant the use of ultrasound by Sikhs and Hindus and in consequence abortions have increased. Suicide is not permissible since life is a gift from God and euthanasia should only be thought of when relatives realise that they can do no more for their loved one. Sikhs would not believe in keeping a person alive when there is no hope of any ultimate improvement.[24]

Our short survey of the moral teaching of religions shows that they agree with the Christian principle that life is God-given and therefore sacred. They also agree with what we have seen in previous chapters that intention in killing is important. Some seem to have a more liberal attitude to abortion than others, for example Sikhism, but in Islam abortion can take place only up to seventeen weeks which is not as liberal as the UK or USA. After that it is murder. However, the Indian religions' belief in reincarnation should in general mean a more liberal attitude since the foetus will have another opportunity in the cycle of rebirth. But all of the religions are against abortion on demand. In connection with suicide, it is not acceptable unless it falls into the category of the giving of life rather than the taking of it.

With regard to capital punishment it has been pointed out that in Islam the Sunni follow the law of Moses rather than the Qur'an in accepting stoning to death for adultery. Muhammad enforced this punishment as is seen in the Hadith tradition (*sunnah*) in Islam. But as we noted jurists find it difficult to obtain a confession when this occurs. The just war criteria operate in the religions, but militant groups do not always respect some of the principles. Often they begin with self-defence but it soon develops into aggression. In the future as more and more contact is made with the West it will be essential that the mainstream in each religion controls such militancy.

Every religion develops in context and the 'global village' has meant being faced with modernity and secularism. How this will increasingly affect attitudes to the issues which we have discussed remains to be seen.

Questions for discussion

- What similarities and differences do you see in the moral traditions of the religions?
- The religions lay down rules or moral principles. How far should we accept these or seek to evolve our own rules in dealing with the issues considered in this book?
- What religion do you think would be most strict with regard to these issues?

- The doctrine of double effect appears to be acceptable to Buddhists. What criticisms can be made of this doctrine?
- All religions have been involved in wars to a greater or lesser extent. How far have they erred in this?

SEVEN

Is Life Meaningless?

The issues which we have discussed in the previous chapters make us stop and think about the meaning of life in general. When parents stand at the grave of a son or daughter who has committed suicide, or the relatives of the victim of a brutal murder agonise over their loss, or a mother wrings her hands in despair when she learns of the death of her son in a seemingly senseless war, questions arise: 'What is life really about? Can there be any purpose or meaning in it? Is it really worth living? If there is a good God, how can he permit such things to happen?'

Underlying the various reasons for suicide that we have put forward lies the conviction that the situation is desperate and the point of no return has been reached. Camus was surely right when he said that suicide is judging whether life is or is not worth living. To someone in despair life as a whole has lost its significance and is not worth continuing. Euthanasia too reflects a judgement about life. There seems little point in continuing to maintain life when it has lost its qualitative value. Can there be any purpose in prolonging the life of a patient who is suffering from terminal cancer? Abortion too, as we have seen, is a serious step to take. It is, as Rosalind Hursthouse says, in a unique way a decision about the meaning of life, for it is a decision about the meaning or value of a potential life which is within one's power and, in part, of one's own making. And it is also a decision about the meaning or point or purpose of one's own life, about what one is going to do with it and make of it and of oneself.[1]

These crises in our lives compel us to think about suffering and death in general and raise the larger questions about meaning and purpose, even though in the final analysis we cannot find conclusive answers. But, while these problems acutely raise these big questions for most people, it is apparent that for others such things as boredom, disappointment, failure, depression and accidents and a host of other evils contribute to the feeling that life is not worthwhile. Meaning, and life being considered worthwhile, seem to be connected in some lives. Marlon Brando, despite being a very successful actor, once testified to a feeling that something was wrong with his life. He believed he felt this way because he had originally wanted to be a writer rather than an actor. Leo Tolstoy, having achieved fame as a writer, felt that his goals crumbled before the question: 'Well, and what then?' He turned to religion in order to find meaning in life, but Brando said: 'Life is a mystery and it is an unsolvable one. You just simply live it through and as you draw your last breath, you say: "What was that all about?" '

These statements are significant, for we often think that life derives its meaning from the purposes that we have. Perhaps Brando's dissatisfaction was indeed caused by the thought that his true ambition had remained unfulfilled. But could he really have achieved the same fame as a writer? Here he might well reply that what he sought was not fame but satisfaction and that you cannot equate them.

It does seem that what we do has an effect on how we view life, for many people are bored and frustrated by routine work which they do not find fulfilling. But Tolstoy,

having accomplished what he had wanted to do, was then
afflicted with the question of whether this was all that there
was to life. He was really looking for an overall purpose
to life, and hence his turning to religion. J. S. Mill did not
take that way, but he too was familiar with the kind of
feeling which Tolstoy had. He experienced a mental crisis
at the age of twenty in which he imagined having
accomplished all the goals in life which he had set himself.
Would he then be happy? 'No. At this my heart sank within
me; the whole foundation on which my life was constructed
fell down. All my happiness was to have been in the continual pursuit of this end. The end had ceased to charm,
and how could there ever again be any interest in the
means? I seemed to have nothing left to live for.'[2]

Mill was a Utilitarian who thought that the purpose of
life was the pursuit of happiness. Hence his problem was
not about the meaning of life but about its happiness. Yet
there appears to be a connection between meaning and
happiness, for if I am continually unhappy I will raise
questions about what life means.

The question is so complicated that some linguistic philosophers have doubted that it has a meaning! The meaning
of meaning has occupied a lot of their time. Fortunately
we need not enter that minefield, for their discussions have
been subjected to strong criticism and recent philosophical
analysis has concluded that the question is intelligible and
that we can discuss it in the context of everyday use.[3]

In this chapter we propose to consider those who for
various reasons contend that they cannot see any meaning
in life. The experience of frustration, suffering and death
leads them to that conclusion. We cannot easily dismiss
their case for, as we have seen, suffering is very prevalent
in the world. Other philosophers, despite recognising that
there is much that is tragic in life, maintain that it has a

meaning and that the meaning can be found within our experience. They try to analyse the nature which we possess and argue that if we knew what man was really like, we could then produce a recipe by which to live. The good life – attained by rationality, the pursuit of happiness and living in harmony with society (or avoiding its corruption by withdrawal to the life of nature) – can give meaning to our lives. At least this is the claim which is made.

Whatever perspective we decide to adopt will have an effect on how we view life in general and will thus influence the way in which we view the issues which we have discussed in previous chapters.

LIFE HAS NO MEANING

Various philosophers of both the past and the present, reflecting on the kind of experiences that we have described throughout this book, conclude that life is meaningless or absurd. We now review aspects of their thinking.

Arthur Schopenhauer (1788–1860) was born in Danzig. His father wanted him to become a banker but he decided to study and lecture on philosophy. Unfortunately, his teaching met with little success. He was embittered by this and became envious of other philosophers who were applauded for their work. It was only in later life that his fame grew and he tasted some success. With regard to life he sounds a very pessimistic note. The world, he said, resembles a penal colony and its inmates – these creatures that we call men – are grotesque. Death is a tragedy. What can we do? Schopenhauer calls for a repression of our desires for power and possessions and a retreat to a desert or a monastery. Here he resembles what we have seen in connection with Buddhism.

The cause of our striving, according to Schopenhauer, is

a purposeless Will which is in us and makes us aim at useless and unsatisfying goals. He arrived at that conclusion because he noticed that striving or Will is to be found in everything. The heart of the universe is Will. But life has death as its goal, and this shows how meaningless it is. For if life had meaning it would not have non-being as its end. Will is the basis of all evil and makes human beings self-centred. He behaves like a wolf and most societies are tyrannies. There is more pain than pleasure in the world, and most of what we experience leads to boredom. How could a good God have created such a world? All the evidence points to a purposeless Will. With regard to suicide he wavers between contending that we should be free to commit it without obstruction by the law or Christianity and arguing that committing the act would be to give in to this blind Will. Not only is this difficult to understand, but also Schopenhauer makes the mistake of thinking that Christianity makes suffering the purpose of life. This is obviously incorrect. It recognises the fact of suffering but argues that belief in God's purposes will overcome it. Christ himself said that he had come to give life abundant (John 10:10). Schopenhauer thinks that suffering is part of the blind Will behind all things, and that we must not be driven by our trouble to choose to be liberated from it by death. Such a victory over the Will, he believes, is a high act of morality and could lead to union with God.[4]

Other philosophers have agreed with Schopenhauer that life is boring for various reasons. One is the cyclic nature of life. It resembles the myth of Sisyphus, who spent his days pushing a boulder up a hill only to see it roll down again. Our days are spent in monotonous routine, and the ceaseless round is perpetuated by our children.

Both Albert Camus and Thomas Nagel, writing in the twentieth century, describe life as absurd. For Camus this means that there is an absurd contrast between what we want in life and what it offers. If we want something really badly and cannot get it we may commit suicide. But the refusal to face life's denials is just as bad as seeking comfort in religion, which is irrational. The best attitude is defiance. Shake a fist at life! This restores our dignity. What makes life so absurd is our lack of knowledge of it. For science, the new god, is full of poetry and metaphor and does not enable us to apprehend the world. The human situation is full of suffering and death, and reason cannot find the way to God.

But is there any conceivable world that would satisfy our desires and demands? Thomas Nagel raises this question in a criticism of Camus, but sees life as absurd in a comic sense. A situation is absurd when there is a discrepancy between aspiration and reality: 'Someone gives a complicated speech in support of a motion that has already been passed; a notorious criminal is made president of a major philanthropic foundation; you declare your love over the telephone to a recorded announcement; as you are being knighted, your pants fall down.'[5] We need to see that many of the situations in life which we take so seriously and earnestly are comical and open to doubt. At times we do see this, but we continue to take our goals too seriously. This sets up a conflict within us. The solution is to handle our aspirations with a degree of irony. Camus' answer, rebellion, is in Nagel's view romantic and self-pitying.

Another difficulty which makes life meaningless is the loss of a sense of an overall purpose, which traditionally was supplied by religion. The scientific world-view, in which the universe is a mechanism obeying the laws of natural cause and effect, rules out any supernatural or transcendent factor such as God. Science, while explaining how the world works, does not appear to have much to say about why it is as it is and what meaning may lie behind it.

But some philosophers such as Kurt Baier insist that it is Christianity which robs us of purpose. Science shows, he thinks, that there is no purpose allocated to human beings from an outside agency. Its findings contradict the traditional religious view of creation and redemption. But Christianity's view of human beings as mere instruments in the hands of God is degrading and removes any real purpose from life. Baier admits that he has not the necessary theological knowledge to pronounce on the claim that Christianity has adjusted its doctrines to accommodate modern scientific knowledge.

W. T. Stace shows a greater knowledge of how theology has responded to scientific research and points out that it has found new intellectual frameworks. But the difficulty remains that science explains matters in terms of cause and effect and has no use for final or teleological causes, which figure prominently in Christian arguments for the existence of God. Science is interested in prediction and control; it can tell us the best way to achieve ends but not what ends to follow. An overall purpose is an illusion and we can live without it.

What criticisms can be offered of this pessimistic view of life? We will consider the question of an overall purpose in the next chapter, but what of other arguments for pessimism? An ironic observation might be that if the world is as bad as Schopenhauer says it is, it is strange that suicide is not more general. But it takes a lot of suffering, hunger and persecution to drive a man or woman to this course of action. We naturally cling to life, hoping that it will get better. Some writers recognise this. Thomas Nagel says, 'life is worth living even when the bad elements of experience are plentiful'. Dmitri Panin makes the same point in a much more telling way when he speaks of the concentration camps: 'I should like to pass on my observations concerning the absence of suicides under the extremely severe conditions of our concentration camps. The more that life became desperate, the more a prisoner seemed determined to hold onto it.'[6]

A more balanced outlook on life in general is that it is a mixture of good and bad, just like human nature itself. Death can be viewed in a more optimistic way. The dying person can be seen as 'a guest retiring gracefully from a meal'. Moreover, when we are old and losing our faculties the approach of death may be a considerable relief to us. But there are deaths – those of infants, children and young people, for example – which seem pointless and cannot easily be dismissed. Some of these can be caused by lack of care or understanding or even by a refusal to have hospital treatment on religious grounds, but there remain deaths which are unexplainable. In such cases there may be some comfort in the thought of an afterlife where explanations may be given and injustices may be righted. But, as we have seen, the pessimists do not believe in immortality. Nor do they believe in any sense of purpose; in their view, life is cyclic and boring. However, Christianity not only believes that there is a purpose within life itself but also claims that there is an overall cosmic plan in which history is moving towards a goal. We will consider whether or not this is conceivable in our final chapter.

Adherents of Christianity and other religions would not accept that their service of God is degrading or lacking in freedom, for they would say that only in the service of an ideal is there perfect freedom. Although he believes in an overall purpose the believer still has the freedom to pursue his own goals, provided they do not conflict with the ethics of his religion. Do not all of us serve some master?

As someone said, 'He was a self-made man and spent all his time worshipping his own handiwork!'

Schopenhauer was wrong when he said the goal of life was death. We have many goals, and most people do not even think of death until the later stages of life or when they are faced with some of the crises we have noted in this book. Life can be boring at times, but we can make routine tasks more interesting by concentrating on something else, and when one goal is achieved we go on to another. It may be that Nagel is right in saying that we take life too seriously. Perhaps we should be more ironic concerning the trials and troubles that afflict us. But while some situations can be treated in that way, we cannot be ironic about suicide, abortion, euthanasia, capital punishment and war. These involve real tragedies. It would seem that Nagel has not acquired the kind of sensitivity which is needed to deal with such situations. Irony is hardly applicable to life as a whole.[7]

If we take the pessimistic perspective on life, then the whole matter of killing in these crisis situations which we have discussed will be affected, for we normally think of life as a good and of death as an evil. But if life is as bad as some thinkers say it is and has so little quality, then we can take it without regret. Why preserve life if it is so miserable? This view of things would affect our view of the sanctity of life, and more and more arguments could be advanced for setting this principle aside.[8] But as we have seen, life has to be very bad before most people will consider suicide. Also, the principle reminds us not to devalue life.

But the pessimists do awaken us to the miseries of life. It may be that this is a good thing, for most of us are inclined to drift through life in a kind of optimism, and perhaps we become indifferent to the needs of others.

MEANING WITHIN LIFE

The issues and crisis situations which we have described in previous chapters arise because of various factors, but we are conscious that in each of them something has gone wrong. Suicide, abortion, euthanasia, capital punishment, war – could it be that the thing which all these issues have in common is the failure of individuals or nations to conduct their lives properly or follow moral rules? War occurs when a leader covets another land; murder takes place because of jealousy, hatred or lust. Amid the various reasons and circumstances which are put forward to justify these acts is the problem of human nature and how we can control our desires and conduct our lives properly. Is there any way of knowing what we are really like and of acquiring the sort of character which will enable us to cope when we are faced with the crucial problems of life?

Philosophers have not been reluctant to describe the essential nature of men and women and how we might realise our best potential. Oswald Hanfling sets out in detail how various philosophers from Aristotle (384–322 BC) to Sartre (1905–1980) have put forward their recipe for the good life and the path to self-realisation which would give meaning to our lives. In summary, they have argued that human beings are rational, socially orientated, inquisitive, aesthetic, moral and playful and that they seek happiness.[9] We shall make some comments on each of the philosophers which Hanfling deals with.

Since it is apparent that something has gone wrong with the thinking of a murderer or a dictator who goes to war, the advice of Aristotle that our mental capacities must be developed properly is well worth taking. He contended that we realise the good life by intellectual activity combined with periods of public service. This immediately raises the problem that some people are not good at rational thinking, especially the sort of thinking which the Greeks often stressed – that is, mathematics. Further, feelings and the will play an important part in our acting morally. Though I must know the good in order to do it, it does not follow that knowledge will lead to performance: 'The good that I would, I do not, and the evil that I would not do, that I do ...' (Romans 7:19). The apostle Paul seems more realistic here than the Greeks.

On the other hand, Aristotle had a great influence on the development of Christian doctrine and ethics. One of the reasons for this was his stress on the development of character traits and virtues which would enable a person to act properly in the crisis situations of life. Prominent virtues were courage, honesty, generosity, justice, public-spiritedness and kindness. To possess these was to possess not only *eudaimonia* (happiness, success) but also wisdom in making difficult decisions. Such a person will not act selfishly but with kindness and generosity towards, for example, the foetus in her womb. It will be a courageous decision which may mean going against circumstances and the advice of others who think lightly about such an issue. It will be a calculating act, recognising (here we see Aristotle's famous doctrine of the mean) that generosity steers a middle course between meanness and indulgence.

There were defects in Aristotle's teaching – for example, he regarded women and slaves as inferior. Kant said his ideal of the virtuous man resembled a character drawn from romantic fiction. However, his stress on developing a good character is helpful, for without such character major problems are difficult to cope with. Also, it is difficult to contest that the development of our intellect is an important factor not only for happiness but also for understanding the meaning of life. Rosalind Hursthouse thinks that the teaching of Aristotle and neo-Aristotelianism, with its stress on character, has much to contribute to a woman's thinking when she is faced with abortion. A woman having such a character will not demand abortion for trivial reasons but because she is sensitive to the suffering of a disabled child or for other good reasons.[10]

Rousseau (1712–1778) placed emphasis on feeling rather than reason. With a full use of the imagination, in his writings he painted a picture of the noble savage and contrasted him with the clever, unscrupulous and vain inhabitant of our modern societies. Culture and civilisation have corrupted our nature, which in its original primitive state was virtuous. The savage was wild rather than wicked, a stranger to vanity, deference and esteem. But as soon as people mingled in society there was inequality, envy, pride and contempt. The purpose of the savage is only to live and be free from labour once needs are satisfied, but civilised people pursue honour, power and wealth.

Despite being idealised and inaccurate, the picture of life in a primitive state that Rousseau draws has its attractions for modern men and women. The rat race, the pollution of our cities and the pursuit of money and power are only some of the things that make us want to escape and lead what we call the simple life of the rustic. Rousseau's concern about the inequalities in modern society anticipated Marx's writings. He would have said that some of the crisis problems which we have considered in this book arise from the ownership of property and the inequalities which it creates. He wrote:

> The first man who, having enclosed a piece of land, thought of saying, 'This is mine', and found people simple enough to believe him, was the true founder of civil society. How many crimes, wars, murders: how

much misery and horror the human race would have been spared if someone had pulled up the stakes and filled in the ditch and cried out to his fellow-man: 'Beware of listening to this imposter. You are lost if you forget that the fruits of the earth belong to everyone and that the earth itself belongs to no one.'[11]

Rousseau neglected the fact that there seems to be something wrong with our natures. We cannot altogether blame our plight on the environment which we have created. And, of course, there was evil in the primitive society as well as in the cities which were eventually created. Still, such creations increase the temptations to which we are prone and they often reduce the value and dignity of the individual. To read Rousseau is to recover a belief in the individual's worth and dignity. Such a belief could give us a better perspective on the life and death issues which we have considered. Modern technology has not only increased the quantity of life but has tended to stifle the natural feelings of sympathy which Rousseau's noble savage had for others.

But the original state of humanity, whatever that was, cannot be recovered. Rousseau himself recognised that there was no going back to it. John Stuart Mill (1806–1873), whose Utilitarianism we have examined, was more realistic about human nature. He recognised the evil in us and pointed to the savagery of non-human nature, where every day there is the kind of killing for which people are hanged or imprisoned. Mill argued that human nature needed to be changed and that education was the way. The purpose of life was the pursuit of happiness, and he tried to widen the meaning of this term, distinguishing the lower pleasures of the body from those of the mind. He argued that only those who had experienced both types of pleasure could judge which was best. Of course, in his view intellectual pleasures were best. But can we make such a separation between body and mind? Does not the one affect the other? Sex is a lower pleasure of the body, but the appropriate frame of mind is required if it is to be really pleasurable. Further, as Richard Norman says, the Utilitarian slogan 'Live for happiness' really means 'Live for whatever you think is worth living for'. How do we know what is worth living for? Utilitarianism fails to provide a focus for our lives around which everything else can revolve. But in his developed thinking Mill does argue for the full realisation of all our faculties. Here he is answering the need of many people who see no meaning in life and are bored because they don't use them or have not had the opportunity to employ them.[12] But, as we have seen, taking up a Utilitarian perspective on the moral problems which we have discussed raises all kinds of difficulties. This philosophy, which is based on the principle of the greatest happiness of the greatest number and which judges an action by its consequences, could justify suicide, euthanasia, abortion, murder and war in ways that those who contend that killing is intrinsically wrong could not tolerate.

With the exception of Rousseau, the thought of the philosophers we have considered so far indicates that society is important in the moral development of our nature and the realisation of the good life. In the nineteenth century F. H. Bradley fully stressed this, arguing not only that we are part of the whole but also that society puts us in a certain place or station. Life takes on meaning if we function well in that position. We are born into a web of relationships: child/parent, employee/employer, citizen/state, language/country. Bradley wrote: 'It is the community which is the true moral organism, and individuals owe their individuality to it, rather than the community being a sum of individuals.'[13] Education will be a key factor here. Morality is relative to a particular society, the individual conscience is not to be trusted and the accumulated wisdom of a community is our guide.

Bradley reflects the 'upstairs, downstairs' mentality of his century. He does not take into account, as Marx did, the fact that societies can be corrupt and that even sacred institutions such as the Church require at times the protest of a Luther to recall them to their ideals. Bradley's view of the relational nature of a person is important but, as he came to realise himself, a lot of evil can enter into a society, and in any given community there are different moral codes which act and react upon individuals.

In sharp reaction to the idea that societies make us what we are, Sartre (1905–1980) contended, as we have seen, that we make ourselves. It is the individual and his choice which is important, not the community. Existence is prior to essence, that is, our nature is made by our decisions not by any prior constitution which we inherit. Thus the genes or environment do not have any determining effect. Values are made by us, and no code can prescribe for us what we ought to do in any given situation. In reaction to Bradley's view that we are fulfilling a proper purpose when we act in the station of life where we have been placed, Sartre would comment that this would be to treat a person as a thing. We cannot explain a person's behaviour in the same way as we would explain the behaviour of a non-human thing – that is, purely in terms of antecedent causes. Only if 'conditioning' has taken place or the person is mentally ill can we explain it in this way. Human nature is not determined by heredity or circumstances or society; rather, we have the power of free choice.

There is value in this stress on the individual and her freedom, for society often tries to treat us as cogs in a machine. Not to recognise this freedom, Sartre says, is to act in 'bad faith'. We are conscious that we can rebel against the role which we play in society, and we ought to. Otherwise we are accepting that we are just a thing. Being sincere is transcending nature, codes and regulations and choosing what we know we should choose. But how are we to know what is the right thing to choose? Existentialism becomes somewhat vague at this point, and sometimes Sartre's characters end up by tossing a coin! There are basic needs which we all have, and one is to have a job so that we can eat and have a home. These factors compel a person to become, for example, a waiter. His decision to become one, as Oswald Hanfling points out, is different from a choice involving moral values, such as whether to join the Communist Party.

Our freedom is relative, not absolute, for we are born into a society with traditions and laws, and we cannot easily set these aside. Values exist apart from what we decide. In brief, while existentialism has a healthy respect for human freedom and shows that the decisions we make can make or mar the meaning of life for us, it does not offer us a standard by which we can live. We are still puzzled as to how to get such a standard.

But whatever the right way to find meaning within life may be – whether it is to lead a life of reason or pleasure or social activity, or to function in our place in society, or to know that we are free to make authentic choices, or to get back to nature – we do know that we are creatures of purpose. Indeed, that may be the problem. Moritz Schlick speaks of being 'cursed by purposes'! He stresses that instead of always striving towards some goal we should do something for its own sake and carry it through in the spirit of play. By so doing we avoid the sense of meaninglessness which we feel when an aim is accomplished as well as when it fails in its outcome. Schlick is right, since we often lose our youthfulness and enthusiasm and become too serious about our concerns. In the games that we play there is order and structure; this appeals to us, because it is unlike the confusion, stress, disorder and tragedy of life. Hence, if we project the spirit of play as far as we can into all kinds of activities, we are more likely to find life more satisfying. Getting fun out of what we are doing relieves the boredom of tasks that must include routine work. However, some work is so tedious that it may be difficult to view it as fun.

Thus in various ways the thinkers whom we have looked at in this section seek to find a purpose within life, recognising that we have goals and ends and that this is characteristic of human beings. But while our attitude to life in general requires a saving sense of humour, does this have anything to contribute to the situations which we have considered in preceding chapters? Perhaps it could be argued that the suicidal person is taking things too seriously and that irony or humour might save his or her life. But, as we have seen, the reasons for suicide go very deep; an ironic attitude could display a lack of sensitivity not only on our part in considering the act but also in the mind of the suicidal person. If the point is to regard life in general in a playful way, this then appears more reasonable, but it is the tragic situations of life which raise the problem of suffering.

Another point that might be worth making is that if human beings are characterised by goals and purposes, we would expect that the Creator, if there were one, would also order the world according to some grand design. But philosophers refuse to take this step because they go along with the scientific view of the world, which stresses the insignificance of humanity and claims that the universe was the result of an accident. Evolutionary theory rules out a special act of God in creation, and the human species is regarded as the outcome of a blind process of selection by survival. Causal explanation (natural cause followed by natural effect) has replaced the old idea that we could explain something by saying what it was for – that is, what purpose it served for human beings or God. In other words, teleological explanation has been replaced by the causal. Of course, not all philosophers accept that scientific explanation can rule out human purposes, for as our discussion has clearly shown, people are no less purposeful today than they used to be. But scientific explanation does appear to undermine the view that the world has an overall purpose or design.[14]

In addition to the modern scientific picture there is also the problem of evil and the loss of belief in a life after death which might adjust the injustices of this world. Taken together, these issues raise major problems for belief in a Creator who made the world and all things in it for a purpose. In the next chapter we will examine these questions and ask if the Judaeo-Christian belief in such a Creator and such an overall purpose for the world can be maintained today. But since these are major areas of debate between theology, science and philosophy, the discussion will have to be concise and somewhat limited in extent.[15]

Questions for discussion
- In the light of the issues discussed in previous chapters are there good reasons for describing life as 'absurd' or 'meaningless'?
- Compare the various views of the good life outlined in this chapter. Which one appeals to you and why?
- According to Aristotle if you want to be a success or

flourish in the best sense you must practise the virtues of benevolence, justice, honesty, generosity etc. Do you think that a person with a character formed by such practice would know what to do when faced with a decision regarding abortion?

EIGHT

What about an Overall Purpose?

Shakespeare was sure there was 'a divinity that shaped our ends, rough-hew them as we will', and Tennyson spoke of a 'one far-off event to which the whole creation moves'.[1] Has science removed such ideas of purpose on the part of a Creator and made everything the result of chance and blind laws? We take up this question first of all, then the problem of evil, and finally the issue of the immortality of the soul.

Isaac Newton (1642–1725) embraced a mechanistic view of the world and required God only to create and carry out repairs from time to time. God controlled all by fixed and immutable laws. Apart from physics, Newton spent a lot of time on theological writing. It is estimated that a third of his literary output was in that area. He accepted the argument that the design in the universe showed that there was a Designer. But philosophers such as Hume and Kant, while treating the argument with respect, were not convinced that it proved the existence of God. Hume believed that it suggested rather than proved. Kant preferred to present the moral argument for God's existence. God, according to Kant, cannot be known by reason, but we do find inherent in reason what he called the categorical imperative. This is the maxim that we should only act when we are sure that we can make our action into a universal law – that is, when we know that everyone would be able to follow what we had done. To so live is deserving of happiness, but often we see the good person suffering and the evil one prospering. Consequently justice demands that there must be immortality and a God who will reward such virtue. It is easy to criticise Kant for this proposal, but it remains one answer to the injustices of life which we can point to. Moreover, it does accord with our sense of justice.

But it was the work of Charles Darwin that most forcefully raised the question of whether there was a Designer or Creator. Darwin's theories also challenged the notion that humanity held a special place in the universe. Firstly, the evolutionary theory implied that the biblical account of creation was wrong, for it said that species of plants and animals had not been divinely and individually created but had evolved. Secondly, the mechanism of evolution, waste and struggle, looked more like accident and chance than purpose. Finally, such a mechanism of natural selection was deemed sufficient to account for the emergence of human life; an intervention by God was not required.

Yet, despite this idea of natural cause followed by natural event, Darwin was reluctant to abandon his belief in God. After all, he had been a theological student! With considerable care he weighed up the alternatives:

> There seems to be no more design in the variability of organic beings and in the action of natural selection, than in the course which the wind blows. Everything in nature is the result of fixed laws ... Another source of conviction in the existence of God, connected with the reason and not with the feelings, impresses me has having much more weight. This flows from the extreme difficulty or rather impossibility of conceiving this

immense and wonderful universe, including man with his capacity of looking forward and backward and far into futurity, as the result of blind chance or necessity. When thus reflecting I feel compelled to look to a First Cause having an intelligent mind in some degree analogous to that of man; and I deserve to be called a Theist.[2]

This quotation is significant, for when Darwin considered human beings and their ability to look into the future and set themselves goals to fulfil, he saw that such intelligence and power to reason could be evidence of the existence of a Higher Mind in the universe. What Darwin is saying here could be put in religious terminology for, according to Scripture, humankind was made in the image of God (Genesis 1:26). This means that human beings reflect in some way their Creator. If human beings behave rationally, we can expect the Creator to be rational, and so on. Now, according to Darwin, humankind is the crown of the evolutionary process, so while its origin and development, which the biologist studies, are very important, it would seem that the study of the characteristics of human beings as they now are may give us a greater understanding of the meaning of life. We shall return to this point later.

Darwin's theistic view, which was strong when he wrote *The Origin of Species* (1859), gradually weakened and he became an agnostic. Why? He had doubts about the human mind being able to draw theistic conclusions; after all, it had developed from the animals. As he said, 'a dog might as well speculate on the mind of Newton'. As far as he was concerned, 'the mystery of the beginning of all things is insoluble by us . . .' But in addition to the struggle for existence in nature he had other reasons to doubt, and these were connected with his study of the Bible. His doubts grew regarding miracles, the reliability of the Gospels and the doctrine of eternal damnation. But doubts had been expressed about these matters before Darwin by clerics who had still remained within the Church. Darwin appears to have been a literalist with regard to Scripture interpretation, and as he says himself, the officers of the *Beagle* laughed at his orthodoxy. His decision to reject the above doctrines was on the basis of 'the plain language of the text'. This literalism surfaces again in his *Autobiography* written five years before his death. It is by taking the passages that refer to hell literally that he denies such a 'damnable doctrine' and moves away from Christianity. He also records that he lost the sense of awe when confronted with the beauty of nature and his desire for anything artistic. His wife warned him of the danger of concentrating so much on the scientific and neglecting other ways of knowing: 'May not the habit in scientific pursuits of believing nothing till it is proved, influence your mind too much in other things which cannot be proved in the same way, and if true are likely to be above our comprehension?'[3] However, the Church has always recognised that Scripture is full of metaphors, similes and myths, and many of the Greek Fathers provided allegorical interpretations. In the event, after an initial confrontation with Darwinism, the Church accommodated its theology to the theory of evolution by arguing that it could have been the process used by the Creator. In 1882 Darwin was buried with honour in Westminster Abbey. Dean Farrar, in the funeral sermon, said that Darwin was not a materialist but a 'healthy, noble, well-balanced wonder of a spirit, profoundly reverent, kindled with deepest admiration for the works of God'.[4]

Darwin postulated both laws of development and random variations. He seemed to waver between seeing the laws as implying a lawgiver and seeing everything as happening by accident. Newton was sure that the existence of laws did indicate a lawgiver, and at one point Darwin did not exclude God as the primary cause, with natural laws being the 'secondary means' by which God created. But looking at the theory of evolution in general, one can see that it tends to portray law as blind and purposeless.[5]

This the theists had to challenge, and found hope in the new model of the cosmos, which thought of it as more like an organism than a machine. In such an evolving universe there is the emergence of new levels of organism; matter evolves into life which evolves into mind. And organisms themselves have higher and lower levels. Even an animal can be regarded as more than a collection of physical and chemical reactions. A certain creative activity is discernible, for the animal can change both its environment and its feeding habits. Further, in seeking to understand the animal it is necessary to examine not only the parts but also the creature as a whole. Physiologists can examine the parts – the circulatory system, for example – but they cannot explain the whole in terms of these. Again, the survival of an animal does not rest only upon its physical make-up but also on its behaviour. In some senses the higher animals appear to be able to 'choose' – that is, an element of will is involved. Thus it is argued that if consciousness plays a real part in the evolutionary process and if the end-products are conscious creatures capable of understanding their own development, then it is difficult to conclude that the whole process is blind.

According to the neo-Darwinists we are the outcome of a number of accidents; our ultimate ancestor was some accidental conjunction of molecules in a primeval oceanic soup. The only guide in the process of accidents which has led from amoeba to human being has been natural selection. To explain something we need to reduce it to its parts, and this has enabled scientists to be very successful in understanding the nature of things. But it is not the complete explanation. A living organism, as John Davy says, can function because a coherent pattern is imposed on the parts of which it consists – the organs are subservient to the organism, the tissues serve the organs, the cells serve the tissues, proteins and other substances serve the cells. There are higher and lower levels and the higher ones control the lower ones. For example, the cells round a wound stop growing when it is healed. But if the cells cannot be controlled they bring illness, anarchy and death.

How is this ordered functioning, in which the whole controls and is more important than the parts, to be explained? Davy sees in this a reminder of the old argument for a Designer as put forward by Paley. The parts of a watch are assembled in a coherent pattern which allows us to tell the time. No investigation of the parts explains the important feature of time telling; this requires a consideration of the watch as a whole. No naturalistic explanation has been found for the design that is there in organisms and in the process of evolution as a whole. Mechanistic explanations are not sufficient.[6]

Karl Popper underlined this when he spoke at the World Congress of Philosophy at Brighton in 1988. He rejected the idea that all causation is 'push' and the determinism which extends to humankind as a result of this idea. He pointed out that Heisenberg's theory of indeterminacy had made the clockwork picture of the universe imprecise. Despite Einstein's protests, Heisenberg's theory had been shown to be the true nature of our world and not simply our subjective impression of it. Now we have the mathematical probability theory, which for one thing implies propensity. This theory points to a world which has an open future and is not a closed deterministic system. This propensity is inherent in things and enables them to realise a goal. New possibilities or emergents arise which are not predictable on the basis of past cause and effect. As Popper said:

> The old world picture that puts before us a mechanism operating with causes that are all in the past – the past kicking us and driving us with kicks into the future – the past that is gone – is no longer adequate to our indeterministic world . . . It is not the kicks from the back, from the past, that impel us, but the attraction, the lure of the future and its attractive possibilities that entice us; this is what keeps life – and, indeed, the world – unfolding.[7]

Popper does not rule out chance but couples it with the preferences of organisms and their ability to achieve possibilities. It would seem that, particularly in explaining human beings, we need to take into account not only antecedent causes but also teleological ones. Hence, while we cannot explain the mystery of the origin of life, we are becoming more aware of order and design in our universe which can be set over against chance and randomness.

Paul Davis points out how marvellous that order is. It was there at the beginning; indeed, we know that order has decreased in our universe. If the universe had been an accident there would have been little chance of it containing order at all, for order can be replaced by or give way to chaos, but not vice versa:

> If the big bang was just a random event, the probability seems overwhelming (a colossal understatement) that the emerging cosmic material would be in thermodynamic equilibrium at maxim entropy with zero order. As this was clearly not the case, it appears hard

to escape the conclusion that the actual state of the universe had been 'chosen' or selected somehow from the huge number of available states, all but an infinitesimal fraction of which are totally disordered. And if such an exceedingly improbable initial state was selected, there surely had to be a selector designer to 'choose it'.[8]

The most likely choice would have been a 'black hole' for matter rather than a star. Davis contends that what is happening in our universe is a gigantic competition between the vigour of the big bang and the force of gravity which tries to pull the pieces together again. What is amazing is the delicate balance involved here. If the big bang had been weaker it would have fallen back on itself in a big crunch, but if it had been stronger the cosmic material would have dispersed so rapidly that galaxies would not have been formed. Matching and uniformity do point to a Designer, but there are no scientific proofs. However, one intriguing development has been the discovery of the singularity, or the outer limits of the natural universe: 'At a singularity, matter may enter or leave the physical world, and influences may emanate therefrom that are totally beyond the power of physical science to predict even in principle. A singularity is the nearest thing that science has found to a supernatural agent.'[9]

Science and religion do use different methods to arrive at the truth about the world. Often it is said that science is concerned with *how* the world works and religion with *why* there is any world at all. But increasingly scientists, following Einstein, are asking *why* as well as *how*.[10] What we have seen is that the way scientists interpret the world does affect religion. The natural and human sciences influence what religion says about humanity and its place in the universe, and the theologian needs to pay attention to this fact. But science proceeds by observation and experiment while religion is based on revelation and religious experience. The two methods are not totally dissimilar, for the first followers of Christianity, Islam and Buddhism observed the behaviour of their religions' founders and experimented with the kind of life that they offered. Indeed it has often been argued that the greatest test of the adherents of any religion is their conformity to the ethics of their founder. Religion also notes that there is more to the scientific method than observation and experiment – there is also the forming of theories. The careers of Darwin and Einstein indicate that often flashes of insight or intuition play a crucial part. Perhaps this phenomenon bears similarities to religious revelation.

While religion, then, cannot base its ideas on the latest scientific finding or argue that God will fill up the gaps in scientific knowledge, it can find encouragement in the fact that the science of today cannot rule out the possibility of a transcendent Ground of all things who may have a purpose for humankind. But what of the immensity of this universe with its black holes and innumerable stars and planets? How can the Creator be interested in such an insignificant speck as a human being? One answer is that we need to judge matters not in terms of quantity but rather in terms of quality, and that it is human beings who have discovered all this about the universe in which they live. What is remarkable is that out of all the planets this is the most suitable for humankind and that so far we have not discovered life on any other. While the earth is no longer regarded scientifically as the centre of the universe, these facts give it a centrality which must make us think that it retains its importance in the eyes of a Creator. But if such a Being exists, how in the face of the problem of evil can we be sure of his benevolence?

THE PROBLEM OF EVIL

While the findings of science and intellectual arguments for the existence or non-existence of God have their place, it is the experience of life itself that often convinces people that there is no cosmic purpose. Earthquakes, famine, disease and the whole range of crises mentioned in this book appear to militate against the idea of a benevolent Being with a good purpose for us. The task is to explain not only natural evil but moral evil as well.

The nature of our answers is often related to our view of the world. Some see it as a battlefield in which we struggle with evil and thus develop character. Adversity, it is said, enables humankind to achieve moral goodness in a way they would not have been able to do if the world had been a playground. But there are other attitudes: there is Camus shaking his fist in rebellion; there is resignation; and, as we saw in the chapter on euthanasia, there is a feeling of being degraded. On the other hand, suffering can arouse compassion in many people, and they become willing to devote their lives to relieving it.

But there is a suffering which seems to be out of all proportion. In our century we recall the death of six million Jews in Nazi concentration camps. The Jews in their history do appear to have had an unparalleled experience of pain: enslavement in Egypt, the wilderness wanderings, the wars of conquest, the experience of exile, the loss of their land, the anti-Semitic persecutions and the holocaust. Yet, according to the Old Testament record, they were the people chosen by God to work out his purpose for the world. Such an election was not a privilege in the sense of favouritism but a burden of responsibility which tested their faith to the utmost. The Old Testament contains many protests and signs of rebellion, and sometimes the Jews made ironic comments on the way they felt God was treating them. Examples of such irony are the saying that it would have been better if God had chosen someone else and the statement found in the rabbinic *midrash* that God offered his law (*Torah*) to all the other nations first and they all rejected it. Israel was God's last hope!

One of their explanations for suffering was that the person must have sinned, and this teaching was still evident in New Testament times. With regard to a certain man who had been born blind the disciples asked Jesus whether he or his parents had sinned. But Jesus dismissed the idea that past sin was the reason for his suffering (John 9:2). Judaism had other explanations: suffering is a test as in the case of Abraham (22:1–19) and the individual's agony must be seen in the light of the total design. Job was chided for his limited knowledge of the design of God (Job 38.4). Islam believes that Allah does all things so suffering must come from Him (Qur'an, lxiv.ii, iii.134). The suffering is a test of faith and helps to reveal character. Buddhism as we noted insists that desires lie at the root of suffering; we must become detached from them. And Hindus believe that suffering is the essence of the universe; there is no escape from it. But in Jewish history another explanation for suffering began to emerge, and that was that God himself suffered with his people. This concept of a suffering God reached its culmination in Christian belief about the crucifixion of Jesus. But the idea of God suffering also sustained many Jews in the awful experience of the holocaust, though many did lose their faith. Another idea which emerged in Jewish history was that the guilty would be punished and the sufferers would be given hope by God in the future.

The Nazis were punished at Nuremburg and elsewhere and the founding of the state of Israel provided the Jews with new hope. But the question remains: Is there any punishment in the world capable of compensating for the crimes that were committed against them?

Why did God permit such suffering? This raises the problem of the power of God and our conception of it. If we say that he is all-powerful, then he must not be good, for if he were he would stop evil. But if he is all-good, then he must lack power, for evil continues. Plato saw God as limited and struggling with unmanageable material. Both Mill and Hume tended to think of God as a finite deity who was limited in his control over evil. But does that not follow from a wrong picture of power? It is the human picture which depicts God as an oriental monarch, master of all that he surveys. But if Jesus has revealed what God is like, then his power is more persuasion than force. If God created the universe, then he gave humankind freedom of will, for without it human beings could not attain responsibility. By creating such a creature God limited himself, but this limitation is not a defect, since it was not imposed upon him. To those who say that God should have made a happy world the Hebrew answer is that he did, but human beings spoiled it by the misuse of their freedom.

Religion has always recognised that there is mystery surrounding God's dealings with us, and sometimes it has retreated in the face of rational argument into this safe harbour. But, as we have said, the Hebrews questioned and in the stories of the fall of humanity which we have in the opening chapters of the Book of Genesis they tried to provide an explanation. They told the stories because they were puzzled by the evil which they saw in themselves and others and could not imagine that a good God would create people with evil in their hearts.

Human beings were created in the image of God, which meant that they were in some way a reflection of their Creator and dependent upon him. But they aspired to break free from this control, thinking that they could become like God. Having made this attempt and failed, Adam became aware of his guilt and tried to blame not only the woman but also God, for it was God who had given him the woman! Whilst most commentators agree that we are not dealing with scientific truth in these narratives, they do seem to be conveying some psychological insights about behaviour! If Adam is a symbol for humanity (the Hebrew word *Adam* means 'humankind'), then each person is the Adam of their own soul and soon adds their sin to that of the race.

Other scholars try to give the stories some kind of contact with history. C. S. Lewis believed that God may have used the process of evolution to perfect the animal form that was to be the physical basis of humanity. Then the creature was given self-consciousness and so was able to comprehend itself and the things of beauty around it. Humankind turned to God in trust and obedience and enjoyed fellowship with him. These primitive beings continued in a paradisal state, but sooner or later they fell either through the sin of pride or because evolution took a wrong turn. Lewis' ideas here bear similarities to those of Rousseau. Lewis could have mounted the same kind of argument as Rousseau did about the goodness of the savage, but Lewis would have seen human nature as being corrupted not only by environment but also by something within its being that responded to sin. Grace and help from God is needed to conquer such a nature, and without this power education can accomplish little. Death is interpreted not as physical but rather as spiritual, bringing about a breakdown in the relationship between creature and Creator.

Judaism, Christianity and Islam see sin as disobedience to the law of God and believe that evil has entered the whole creation in this way. Instead of peace, harmony and co-operation there is hatred, violence and 'the survival of the fittest'. But the religious stories do not explain how evil got there in the first place so as to provide a temptation for human beings. In the New Testament there is postulated a superhuman power who has also fallen from grace and tries to ensnare us. In the nineteenth century the Social Darwinians applied the idea of evolution to human moral progress and believed that we would climb steadily higher in the virtues. Some theologians spoke eloquently of 'the fatherhood of God and the brotherhood of man'. The idea that there was a power of evil in the world was ridiculed. However, the twentieth century, with its awful wars and its concentration camps, raised the question once more. How could such a civilised and cultured nation as Germany allow men who behaved as if they were demonic to rise to power?

In some religions such as Zoroastrianism evil forces are viewed as equal with God in power, but most other religions have seen them as subordinated and have believed that their defeat is inevitable. Whatever we think of these ideas, they offer no ultimate solution. But there are hints in Hebrew thinking which are helpful. The Jews thought that God's objective in creating the world was to make humankind happy and that by their own fault human beings ruined things. When we look at what philosophers such as Hume and Mill say, we find that they agree that we should expect happiness but proceed to blame God for the fact that we do not get it. Yet much of the moral evil in the world is due directly to one person's inhumanity to another, and a lot of the natural evil is due to human carelessness and misuse of resources. We blame earthquakes and floods on God, and yet, although we are warned not to live in certain areas because of the danger of tremors, we continue to do so. Deaths due to earthquakes in California and in other parts of the world highlight this refusal to heed the warnings of the geologists. For years they have been warning people about the faults in the earth's surface there, which have caused a number of earthquakes in the past. Major earthquakes in fact occur in well-defined regions. More and more we can cope with disasters, famines and disease if we take care and share our knowledge and resources with the ignorant and needy. Further, the Hebrew/Christian concept of a God who suffers with and for us is not the detached Being of Greek philosophy and indicates a compassion with our lot that does much to help. Self-sacrifice and suffering are at the heart of the Christian doctrine of the incarnation, and there is much comfort in believing that 'in every pang that rends the heart, the Man of Sorrows has a part'.

There is also the thought that the universe is striving towards a goal of some kind – a consummation, a more perfect ideal. In such achievement suffering plays a part, and human beings are called to co-operate with God. Unlike the animals, we are moral beings. Any effort to reach a moral standard demands a struggle and a conquering of our nature. Suffering, then, is necessarily involved. Religion requires us to have trust and faith even when our suffering is undeserved. Christ is the model for the Christian. There is also the hope that the injustice will be set right – if not here, then elsewhere. It is to this hope that we must now turn our attention.

IS THERE LIFE AFTER DEATH?

There are a number of interconnections between the issues discussed in previous chapters but the one thing that connects them all is the fact of death. The belief in life after death does supply some meaning to a life cut short. But many philosophers today think that such a hope is unjustified because they cannot understand how a mind or soul could exist without a body. If there is such an entity as the mind, it needs to function through the brain, which is physical. So how can the mind function without the brain? We shall treat the concepts 'mind' and 'soul' as interchangeable, since they have generally been treated in this way in philosophical discussion. (However, it can be argued that 'soul' unlike 'mind' refers to feeling and willing as well as thinking.) We hope in this section to consider briefly how philosophy has dealt with these concepts and how it has arrived at the various positions which we have today. Then we shall look at the Christian belief that there can be no dualism between soul and body and that immortality will mean a new body.

People have always dreamed during their sleep, so it must have been natural for people in ancient times to believe that their spirits moved around freely without their bodies when they slept. Since the spirit was active during sleep, it must have been easy to believe that it lived on when the body was dead. A common belief was that food and drink must be left near the body in case the spirit wanted to refresh itself. Gradually there developed the idea of transmigration – that is, the belief that at death the soul left the body and made its abode in another. According to Hindu belief, as we have seen, the law of *karma* (deeds done in the former life) determined what position in society the soul would take up. Good deeds could result in an upgrading to a higher caste whereas evil ones meant a poor reincarnation.

The Indians and the Greeks believed in the pre-existence of souls, and the Hebrews and the Greeks thought of immortality in terms of a ghostly and shadowy place. Plato and Greeks in general did not think much of the body but saw the soul as indestructible. Justice demanded that each person should be rewarded or condemned for his deeds on earth, and this required immortality. The soul needed to free itself from the body just as a bird wanted to get out of a cage. Plato in his *Republic* describes the process of education whereby we can gradually emerge from the 'cave' of this world into the light of reason. Mathematical and philosophical study will play a leading role in such emancipation, and we will eventually arrive at a vision of the Good or the perfect Form. True knowledge is recollection of what was clearly known in the pre-existent state; it is not gained by sense observation, which deceives.

The Hebrews did not separate body and soul as the Greeks did, and there is little evidence of any kind of belief in immortality until the Book of Daniel, which was probably written sometime in the second century before Christ. The concept is also found in the Second Book of Maccabees. But there it is the whole person, not simply the soul, which is raised by God to eternal life. This must have had some influence on the fully developed doctrine of the resurrection of the body which emerged in Christianity and which we will discuss shortly.

The Greek view did affect the development of Christian doctrine and philosophy. Descartes argued for a dualism of body and mind and considered that it was the mind which was important. He spent a day on one occasion doubting everything, and at the end of the day he had little to believe in! But then he asked himself the question: 'Is there one thing that I cannot doubt?' His answer immediately was that he had spent the day doubting! I doubt, or better, I think; therefore I am or I exist. It was not a novel conclusion, for Plato, as we have seen, stressed the soul and the need for its education. Descartes argued that since the soul was part of the Whole or part of God, the Absolute Substance, it could not be thought of as disappearing; rather, it continued for as long as God continued. So the soul could not be affected when the body died.

But with the British philosophers Locke, Berkeley and Hume there was more of an attempt to base human knowledge on the senses. For example, Hume argued that all we actually know is what he called 'perceptions' – that is, experience of heat and cold, light and shade, love and hatred, pain and pleasure, and so on. Hence the mind or soul is simply a jumble of perceptions. There is no unifying centre. I only feel that there is a bond, but it cannot be observed. Hume is like the Buddhist who denies that we have a soul. According to the Buddhist the mind is just one of a number of aggregates. To get rid of the delusion of thinking we have a personal centre is to get rid of desire and consequently of the suffering which flows from wanting things. Eliminate desire, and the way to Nirvana is open. Hume tried to work out a theory of personal identity without taking into account other people and their minds. Philosophers argue that this cannot be done. Also, knowledge comes from more sources than just sense observation. For example, memory is very important in establishing to myself and to others who I am. Further, I have thoughts and no observation of my brain will disclose what those thoughts are. Some say that they know what people are thinking by their behaviour, but while this proves correct at times, it is not always so.

Kant was not satisfied with Hume's conclusions but he

admitted that the Scottish philosopher's work awakened him from his dogmatic slumbers! He agrees with Hume that knowledge arises from experience but argues that the mind supplies the form by which we know that experience. Although we cannot by reason prove that there is a self or soul, we may act as if there were one, since there is value in so doing. As we have mentioned before, Kant believes in a moral law which has the soul as its basis. This demands good will. This good will shows itself in our always acting from a sense of duty. A man of good will does not repay a debt in order to avoid punishment, or keep promises because it will benefit him. He performs these acts because it is his duty to do so. Further, before acting he asks the question: What if everybody did this? In other words, can he make his conduct into a universal law? For example, if tempted to steal, he refrains, because he knows that if everybody did this property would not be safe, and this would have a disastrous effect on society. But the man of good will realises that he often fails to achieve his ideal. He knows what the moral law demands but cannot obey it perfectly, for life is too short. Therefore he lives in the faith that there is a life beyond this one, where what he has aimed at will be possible and actual. In brief, Kant's idea of morality demands the immortality of the soul. Kant's viewpoint has been criticised, but it has the virtue of linking the thought of immortality with our moral ideas.

But, after the work of Darwin, human affinities with the animals were stressed and some saw the mind as a mere accompaniment of the material brain processes. With the increased emphasis on observation and experiment in science, it was argued by the advocates of behaviouristic psychology that people knew the thoughts of others by observing their actions. It was dangerous to speculate beyond such observation.

But there are those who contend that the human mind is distinct from the minds of non-human creatures. The use of language, the construction of tools, the size of the brain, the intelligence to survive though opposed by animals which are stronger, bigger and swifter – all these things make humans something special. There is, as the existentialists point out, the freedom to choose, self-awareness and the ability to introspect. While we can infer another's thoughts by watching her actions, we can do this only indirectly and can be mistaken, whereas we know our own thoughts directly. Suppose I am standing in a crowded room and watching a person lifting a glass to her lips. What is she doing and thinking? Is she having a drink for refreshment? Is she drinking poison? Is she celebrating someone's birthday? I cannot tell directly by observation; I need to enter into the whole process of talking with her, and even then she may hold something back. If it were possible for me to examine her brain I still would not be able to detect her thoughts. Let us think of ourselves and take the case of pain. I know it directly; I do not need to make any observations in order to convince myself that I am in pain. But how did I get this pain? Was it something I ate? Or is it the stuffiness of the room? The experts on pain will tell me the cause or try to convince me that I am just imagining it. There are pains for which no bodily cause can be discovered. In the case of liver disorders, pain can be felt in the right shoulder – we could rightly expect it to be felt elsewhere! If we identify pain with a brain process, as the materialist does, then why is it not in my brain but in my right shoulder?[11]

What we can say is that our thinking is related to brain states. This is acceptable both to those who follow Descartes and to those such as Gilbert Ryle who embrace a more sophisticated materialism. The latter position cannot accept survival after death; the former can, but even on this Cartesian basis it does seem that the body would be needed. Since the mind has used the body throughout life, how can it function without it after death?

We shall return to the question of the unity of body and mind in a future state shortly. But does contemporary research offer us any evidence or even any hint of the possibility of such a future state? In recent times considerable data on this subject has been amassed, including accounts of near-death experiences, physical research and claimed memories of former lives. Paul and Linda Badham devote two chapters of their book *Immortality or Extinction?* to examining this data. After considering the arguments for and against, they conclude that there is 'at least some evidence to support the belief in the immortality of the self through bodily death'.[12] Near-death experiences in particular seem relevant, for it might be expected that the nearer we get to an experience the more likely we are to have intimations of it. From the many cases which have been documented by various writers, we select that of the late well-known philosopher, A. J. Ayer.

In 1988, after a bout of pneumonia, Ayer was rushed into hospital, where his heart stopped for four minutes. He was not dead, for, as we have seen, death is connected with the brain stem and not with the stoppage of the heart. He was dying rather than dead. In an article published in the *National Review* of October 1988 he recorded that during these four minutes he saw a red light which he thought was responsible for the government of the universe. He observed two ministers who were in charge of space, but space itself appeared out of joint. He wanted to extinguish the light, but the laws of nature did not seem to be functioning and he was unable to attract the attention of the ministers.

What are we to think of such an experience? According

to those philosophers who wrote the obituary notices when Ayer died a year later, it was an hallucination. This is the customary judgement of those who argue against belief in such experiences. But what did Ayer, who had propounded the empiricist philosophy during a lifetime of teaching and writing, think of his experience? In lucid prose he reflects on some of the mind–body issues that we have been discussing. The easiest answer, he thinks, to the questions of future life would be to say that there may be a prolongation of our experiences without any body. He thinks this view is inconsistent with the concept of personal identity adopted by both Hume and William James. This is that one's identity consists not in the possession of an enduring soul but in the sequence of one's experiences, guaranteed by memory. But the main problem is to discover the relation or relations which have to hold between experiences for them to belong to one and the same self. Ayer himself says that he has not been able to account for personal identity without falling back on the identity, through time, of one or more bodies that the person might successively occupy. He then writes:

> The admission that personal identity through time requires the identity of a body is a surprising feature of Christianity. I call it surprising because it seems to me that Christians are apt to forget that the resurrection of the body is an element in their creed. The question of how bodily identity is sustained over intervals of time is not so difficult. The answer might consist in postulating a reunion of the same atoms, perhaps in their being more than a strong physical resemblance, possibly fortified by a similarity of behaviour.[13]

Ayer points to two important Cambridge philosophers – J. M. E. McTaggart and C. D. Broad – who, though atheists, believed in survival after death. McTaggart derived his view from metaphysics and Broad based his on the findings of psychical research. Since Ayer experienced not God but rather survival, he concludes that it may be possible to have the one apart from the other. The experience may have been a delusion, but then again it may have been true. He writes that his previous conviction that there is no life after death has now been 'slightly weakened' but stresses that there is no need for his friends in the Humanist Association, the Rationalist Press and the South Place Ethical Society to think that he has ceased to be an atheist!

It will be interesting to see how research into near-death experiences develops in the future. In his discussion of personal identity Ayer has drawn our attention to the Christian belief in the resurrection of the body, and we conclude this section with a brief reference to it.

In the history of the Church some thinkers have been influenced by the Greek/Cartesian dualism of body and soul, but biblically they are viewed as a unity. The Bible recognises that the body leads human beings into temptation but teaches that it is essentially good and not something to be punished or escaped from. The resurrection of the body is not the resuscitation of a corpse but the transformation of the physical body into a spiritual one. The apostle Paul discusses this doctrine in his first letter to the church at Corinth and says that he can produce witnesses to the resurrection of Christ. There are difficulties in the gospel narratives in that they do not agree on the specific details of this event. Sometimes Jesus appears to have a physical body and can be touched and recognised. At other times he seems to have a spiritual body; then he is not clearly recognised and can pass through doors. But what the narratives seem to be saying is that there is some relation between the old form of life and the new. Paul uses the analogy of the seed and the plant. The seed dies and the new plant appears; there is a relation between them but also a difference. Paul stresses 'appearances' and denies a 'flesh and blood' formation of the new body (1 Corinthians 15:50). This agrees with the gospel narratives when they indicate that there was a difference about Jesus, so that the disciples did not recognise him. But it conflicts with passages that speak of him as being not a spirit but someone who could be touched and whose body possessed 'flesh and bones' (John 20:27). Various ways of reconciling the conflicting passages have been suggested. One is to say that the resurrection body of Jesus was different from his ascension body; another is to say that some of the gospel writers wanted to materialise what was a spiritual experience. But if such an event as the resurrection of Jesus took place it must have been extremely difficult to describe. It is interesting that the Gospel which is generally regarded as the earliest does not have in its traditional form any description of the resurrection. The appendix to Mark's Gospel (16:9–20) was added later.

Attempts have been made to suggest that these encounters with the resurrected Jesus were hallucinations, but this idea runs into difficulties for a number of reasons. A person needs to be very firmly convinced that he has seen or heard something in order to be willing to die for it. It may be countered that the early Christians were deceived. But this is hardly likely in the case of the 500 'brethren' whom Paul mentions at the beginning of chapter 15 of 1 Corinthians. They were 'witnesses' of the event. But it might still be objected that we are talking about 'primitive' people living in a pre-scientific age in which all kinds of 'wonders' and 'miracles' were believed in. Consequently they would have believed anything! I think we need to be careful here, especially in the case of the apostle Paul, who seems to have been acquainted not only with Hebrew ideas but also with Greek ones. But if the people of Paul's age were 'primitive', then surely they would have believed in the resurrection of Jesus when Paul preached it. Yet the message seems to have caused many riots, if the narrative in the Acts of the Apostles is correct. On one occasion, when Paul presented it to the philosophers on Mars Hill, he was laughed to scorn (17:32). So we can see that the ancient world did not accept it easily.

The historian, of course, cannot investigate such an event, since it brings in a factor that does not figure in her investigations – namely, God. But she can investigate the crucifixion of Christ and the disciples' faith. She will note that with the death of Jesus and the scattering of his band the movement which he had started appeared to be finished. The historian will wonder how such an extraordinary phenomenon as the Church began in these circumstances. When she looks by way of comparison at the founders of other religions she will see that they died peacefully or in a position of prominence, respected not only by their immediate followers but also by their people in general. The historian is bound to conclude that something extraordinary did occur to change frightened men and women into the preachers and witnesses of the early Church.

Such a faith called for trust, and the early Christians felt that they had good reasons for such trust. Paul and other apostles spent a great deal of time arguing for the hope of immortality. They believed that Christ's resurrection was the guarantee of theirs. Paul invited the audiences of Jews and Greeks to whom he preached to weigh up the arguments. Peter advised his converts, 'always ... have your answer ready for people who ask you the reason for the hope that you all have' (1 Peter 3:15). Paul in his Epistles piles up arguments to try and convince Jews and Gentiles of the reality of his message.

What kind of afterlife there will be is open to speculation. There is no question of a life of bliss and idleness such as the one the old washerwoman envisaged when she said, 'I'm going to do nothing for ever and ever!' More likely is a life which will provide answers to the mystery of this one and will involve the pursuit of goals unattainable in this existence. Such a hope comforts many people who suffer and encourages them in this 'vale of tears', but they recognise that the way to that future life is not only trust but also work to alleviate the injustices which are so apparent here.

CONCLUSION

In this book we have been engaged in examining moral problems connected with abortion, capital punishment, murder, war, euthanasia and suicide. If we add to these the problems of suffering in general we might conclude with the pessimists, 'Vanity of vanities, all is vanity' (Ecclesiastes 1:2). The converse of this view is that this is 'the best of all possible worlds', for there is much of beauty, courage and human fellowship in it.

We reject both views in favour of what we consider to be a more balanced and realistic viewpoint – that is, that our experience is a mixture of good and bad. It would seem that our perspective on life is determined not only by our experience of life, with its doubts about any overall purpose, but also by how we are constituted: 'Two men looked out of prison bars; the one saw mud, the other saw stars.'

Most of us do find a focus or centre for our lives, such as our work, our family, our friends, and in pursuing goals related to this we find happiness and pleasure. But suffering in general and the crisis situations we have considered urge us to ask the question about the meaning of life as a whole and to ask whether there is any cosmic purpose. A belief that there is indeed meaning and purpose in life gives us hope in the face of suffering and death. We are also encouraged by the thought that virtue will be rewarded in an afterlife. Religions communicate this hope to their followers but differ in the ways in which they view the world as we know it. Hinduism tends to join with idealistic philosophy in seeing the world as an illusion or appearance; reality lies behind what we perceive. Buddhism and Sikhism speak of being deluded by the world, but Christianity, Judaism and Islam treat it in a realistic way. Of course, some suffering is so intense that it invokes the pessimism of Job or the writer of the Book of Ecclesiastes. The apostle Paul at one point contends that if Christians have hope only in this life, then they are very miserable people. But he reassures his readers by telling them that since Christ has risen from the dead, there is nothing that can separate them from the love of God and that all things work together for good (1 Corinthians 15; Romans 8:28–35).

Concerning the moral problems which have been at the centre of our attention throughout this book, the Christian perspective tries to encourage hope, love, endurance, courage and faith. It willingly embraces the virtues taught by Aristotle which we have outlined but adds the larger hope of life after death. The perspective does not pretend to have all the answers but recognises that God's ways are mysterious; since he is greater than anything we can conceive of, this is bound to be the case. Now 'we see in a mirror dimly . . . now I know in part' (1 Corinthians 13:12).

While Christians hold the Ten Commandments in great respect, they recognise also that Christianity is a religion of love rather than law. Thus when law conflicts with human need, then love or compassion must take priority.

So there are no easy answers when it comes to issues like suicide, abortion, euthanasia and war, and individual Christians will arrive at different judgements.

These judgements will have to stand up to the examination of philosophy so that their rationality may be assessed. Much is to be gained by a dialogue between theology and philosophy on such crucial issues. The early Greek Fathers employed the Platonic philosophy and the work of Aristotle came to figure prominently in the writings of later Christian thinkers. As Rosalind Hursthouse says:

> Subsequent generations of Western moral philosophers have been students of the ancient Greek and Roman moral philosophy, or been Christian; indeed, until very recently, most have been both. Some aspects of Judaeo-Christian morality do not mesh well with ancient Greek ethics, but others have meshed so well that it is now extremely difficult to be clear about which aspects of our moral thinking are genuinely secular and which require a theological backing to make sense. The rather general idea that morality 'applies' to everyone, or that everyone 'ought' to be moral, or has reason to be moral, no matter how 'unnatural' or atypical a human being they are, is doubtless connected (whether one realises it or not) with the Judaeo-Christian idea that no human being can escape God's commands, and with the Christian idea that any human being, no matter how psychologically odd, has an immortal soul which can be saved or lost by acting as virtue requires. But it is also, I suspect, connected (once again, whether one realises it or not) with the Aristotelian idea that the best of life for (nearly) all human beings is the life we live together, practising the virtues to our mutual benefit and enjoyment.[14]

She could also add that there are modern philosophers who accept the Christian ethic but reject the framework of doctrine which lies behind it. But sometimes their criticisms indicate that they do not understand how Christian doctrine has changed and developed over the years and has adapted itself to what science and philosophy are now saying. It is hoped that this book will persuade philosophers to look again at these developments. If this happens, our efforts will have been worthwhile. It is also hoped that those who are struggling with the problems that we have described throughout the book will receive encouragement in the midst of their personal crises and will come to understand that their lives do have some meaning.

Questions for discussion
- Does religion give meaning to life?
- Life is a challenge and struggle, but without these would eternal life be boring?
- How far do scientific claims about the universe and what we are show that life is meaningless?
- Do the problems posed by suicide, euthanasia, abortion, punishment and war militate against belief in God?

Notes

Chapter One

1. A. Giddens, *Sociology of Suicide* (London: Cass & Co., 1971), p. 1327. Cf. C. Varah, *The Samaritans in the '80s* (Constable, 1980). Internet sites are advising on methods of suicide, which is contrary to the 1951 Act which prohibits such a practice. There is a church of euthanasia 'site' listing suicide techniques. It is stated that you can make a final recorded message. See *British Medical Journal*, August 1999, p. 337.

2. Stephen Platt and Norman Kreitman, 'Trends in parasuicide and unemployment among men in Edinburgh 1968–1982', *British Medical Journal*, vol. 289, 20 Oct. 1981.

3. Mike Blank and Jill Fardell, 'The other victim' and 'Those left waiting', *Nursing Times*, 28 June and 4 July 1989, p. 28ff.

4. Derek Humphry and Ann Wickett, *The Right to Die* (London: Bodley Head, 1986), p. 5.

5. Augustine says, however, that we should have compassion on women who have been raped and commit suicide. Judas did not atone for his guilt but increased it by leaving himself no chance of repentance. Christians should not kill themselves in any circumstances, for to kill oneself is to kill a human being. *The City of God*, introduced by John O'Meara (Harmondsworth: Penguin, 1972), pp. 27f. and 30.

6. In the Book of Job there is the suggestion that Job should commit suicide, but he refuses. See attitude to martyrdom in *Early Christian Writings*, ed. Andrew Louth (Harmondsworth: Penguin, 1987). The Council of Carthage in AD 348 condemned suicide.

7. Robert Campbell and Diane Collinson, *Ending Lives* (Oxford: Blackwell, 1988), p. 38; John Donne, *Biathanatos*, ed. E. W. Sullivan II (University of Delaware Press, 1984); David Hume, 'Of suicide' in P. Singer (ed.), *Applied Ethics* (Oxford University Press, 1986), p. 19ff.; J. Bentham, *An Introduction to the Principles of Morals and Legislation*, ed. J. Burns

and H. Hart (Methuen, 1982), ch. 1; J. S. Mill, *Utilitarianism* (Fontana, 1962).

8. J. S. Mill, *On Liberty* (Fontana, 1962), p. 213ff.

9. J.-P. Sartre, *The Reprieve* (Penguin, 1963), p. 309.

10. D. Cook, *The Moral Maze* (London: SPCK, 1989), p. 84.

11. Josephus, *Wars of the Jews*, quoted by William Barclay, *The Plain Man's Guide to Ethics* (London: Collins Fontana, 1973), p. 74. The Japanese in the Second World War engaged in such suicide acts in defence of Iarawa, Peleliu and Iwo Jima. But how are the mass suicides of religious cults in the twentieth century to be viewed? David Koresh's Waco, Texas, cult; Jim Jones' followers in Guyana, etc.?

12. Humphry and Wickett, *Right*, p. 277n. See present writer's discussion of the Ulster crisis in *Loyal to King Billy: A Portrait of the Ulster Protestants* (London: Hurst, 1987).

13. M. P. Battin and D. J. Mayo, *Suicide: Philosophical Issues* (London: Peter Owen, 1980), p. 55.

14. The story of the Jewish patriot is based on an actual person, but I have changed details and the manner of his death to illustrate the difficulty of judging suicide.

15. R. Holland, 'Suicide' in *Talk of God*, Royal Institute of Philosophy lectures, vol. II (1969).

16. Church of England Report, 'Ought suicide to be a crime?' (Church of England Board for Social Responsibility Information Office, 1959), p. 7ff.

17. Quoted by Humphry and Wickett, *Right*, p. 277.

18. Battin and Mayo, *Suicide*, p. 229.

19. BMA Report, 'Euthanasia' (London, 5 May 1988), p. 11.

20. Albert Camus, *The Myth of Sisyphus* (Harmondsworth: Penguin, 1975), p. 11.

21. N. Kreitman and S. Platt, *Current Research on Suicide and Parasuicide* (Edinburgh University Press, 1990). Paul Badham asserts that the suicide rate among doctors is much higher than the general public because they have the means and knowledge to end their lives when they think their position is hopeless; see 'Should Christians accept euthanasia?' in *Euthanasia and the Churches*, ed. Robin Gill (London: Cassell, 1998), p. 51. Recent research apparently opposes the view that high concentration of Catholics in an area means lower suicide rates. It also appears that the fewer religions in any particular state the lower the suicide rates; e.g. research carried out in 1998 by Christopher Ellison at the University of Texas – see Raj Persaud, *Staying Sane* (London: Metro, 1998), p. 430.

22. D. Lamb, *Down the Slippery Slope* (London: Croom Helm, 1988), p. 51.

23. In this respect the Samaritans are an excellent organisation, and they, like others, deserve greater financial support.

24. Campbell and Collinson, *Ending Lives*, p. 114f.

Chapter Two

1. BMA Report, 'Euthanasia' (London, 5 May 1988), p. 19. In the USA the right to die has created debate between relatives, states, doctors and patients. After an exhaustive survey, J. Hoefler and B. Kamoie state that this has resulted in an erosion of trust between patient and doctor, led to a variety of state legislation, and the advance of the 'happy death' movement. There has also been the development of a mediation process. Hoefler and Kamoie, *Deathright* (San Francisco: Westview Press, 1994), chs 4–9. In July 1999 it was reported that a mother had appealed to the courts in the UK demanding that she should be consulted before treatment of her son was ceased. Doctors wanted to let the disabled son die but she refused. She argued that the law should compel doctors to consult parents. The court upheld her appeal. In the UK the possibility of the erosion of trust between patient and doctor (in this case the family GP) was highlighted in February 2000 by the conviction of Dr Harold Shipman for the murder of 15 of his women patients.

2. BMA, 'Euthanasia', p. 19. Statistics show that the majority of doctors do not want active euthanasia (meetings of the BMA in 1992/3/7). Andrew Dennett, *Euthanasia: The Heart of the Matter* (London: Hodder & Stoughton, 1999), p. 46.

3. BMA, 'Euthanasia', p. 69.

4. Duncan Vere, *Voluntary Euthanasia: Is There an Alternative?* (London: Christian Medical Fellowship, 1979). Brian Pollard confirms Vere, but Ruth Russell points to a poll of doctors taken some years ago (the number of doctors polled was 2,000) which showed that 48.6 per cent said that they had been asked by a dying patient for euthanasia. Pollard, *Euthanasia* (Bedford: Little Hills Press, 1989); Russell, *Freedom to Die* (New York: Human Sciences Press, rev. edn. 1977), p. 155. Cicely Saunders of the hospice movement agrees with Pollard and Vere, saying that her patients do not ask for euthanasia.

5. BMA, 'Euthanasia', p. 12. Ludovic Kennedy, in his booklet *Euthanasia* (London: Chatto & Windus, 1990), finds fault with this report. He reflects in his thinking some of the arguments for euthanasia which we have mentioned.

6. BMA, 'Euthanasia', p. 24.

7. BMA, 'Euthanasia', p. 46.

8. James Rachels, *The End of Life* (Oxford University Press, 1986), p. 15ff.

9. Russell, *Freedom*, p. 271.

10. Hugh Trowell, *The Unfinished Debate on Euthanasia* (London: SCM Press, 1973), p. 62. In 1996 it was reported that eight PVS (permanent vegetative state) patients had died in England after the courts sanctioned the removal of feeding tubes, and in Scotland doctors were assured that they would not suffer legal prosecution. But there was recognition in a study published in the *British Medical Journal* that caution was needed in withdrawing treatment as 17 out of 40 patients had been misdiag-

nosed. They later 'woke up'. But according to a survey carried out by the Centre of Medical Law and Ethics doctors favoured withdrawal of treatment even if the patient was likely to recover some degree of consciousness in the future. C. Donnellan (ed.), *Euthanasia* (Cambridge: Independence, 1997), vol. 4, pp. 9, 25, 32. The *British Medical Journal* recommended on 21 August 1999 that a Bill should be introduced in Parliament to regulate mercy killing by doctors which would mean that while euthanasia would remain a crime there would be a statuatory defence for doctors written into the criminal code guaranteeing immunity from prosecution. On 6 December 1999, it was alleged (*Daily Telegraph*) that the NHS was operating involuntary euthanasia. This was denied by a spokesman for the BMA on BBC radio. The debate concerns BMA guidelines which allow withdrawal of food and water for stroke victims who are not terminally ill.

11. Based on various reports by the churches. The Roman Catholic Church has continually opposed voluntary euthanasia, reflected in 1996 when the head of the Catholic Church in Australia said that the first death of this kind under the Northern Territory's Rights of the Terminally Ill Act was a 'shameful day for Australia'. Donnellan (ed.), *Euthanasia*, p. 119.

12. BMA, 'Euthanasia', p. 29.

13. BMA, 'Euthanasia', p. 49f. Compare Richard Fenigsen, *A Case against Dutch Euthanasia* (Hastings Centre Report, 1989, Medical Education Trust, Liverpool). In the Dutch Remmelink Report (1991), 3,000 deaths were attributed to euthanasia. A number of doctors have been prosecuted. In 1996 the number of deaths was approximately 4,000 a year. Donnellan (ed.), *Euthanasia*, p. 16. It was reported in July 1999 that the Dutch government plans to legalise euthanasia. This would give official sanction to a situation which placed doctors in a legal limbo and meant that they were technically committing a crime.

14. BMA, 'Euthanasia', p. 56.

15. BMA, 'Euthanasia', p. 59.

16. A. B. Downing and Barbara Smoker, *Voluntary Euthanasia* (London: Peter Owen, 1986), p. 221.

17. Michael Ignatieff, 'When Hippocrates loses out to Socrates', *Observer*, 22 July 1990.

18. Paul Badham, 'Should Christians accept the validity of voluntary euthanasia?' in Robin Gill (ed.), *Euthanasia and the Churches* (London: Cassell, 1998), p. 42ff. With regard to palliative care in Holland, some say it is advanced but others deny it. Donnellan (ed.), *Euthanasia*, vol. 4, pp. 1, 6.

19. Response by Michael Northcott in Gill (ed.), *Euthanasia*, p. 69ff.

20. Reply by Paul Badham in Gill (ed.), *Euthanasia*, p. 79.

Chapter Three

1. P. F. R. Gardner, *Abortion: The Personal Dilemma* (Exeter: Paternoster Press, 1972), p. 86. Statistics for England and Wales in 1995 show that 90 per cent of abortions were performed under the clause of the Act which allowed it on the grounds that it prevented risk of injury to the physical or mental health of the woman. The 1967 Act did not apply in Northern Ireland, but an Act in 1945 permitted abortion with a clause similar to the one mentioned above. In the Irish Republic, in 1992, an amendment to the law forbidding abortion allowed women to travel abroad for an abortion or to have an abortion at home when the mother's life was threatened. Mary Pipes, *Understanding Abortion* (London: The Women's Press, 1998), pp. 66, 68.

2. Michael Tooley, 'A defence of abortion and infanticide' in *The Problem of Abortion*, ed. J. Feinberg (California: Wadsworth Publishing, 1984), p. 51ff.

3. Tooley, 'A defence', p. 7.

4. Judith Jarvis Thomson, 'A defence of abortion', *Philosophy and Public Affairs*, vol. 1, no. 1 (1971), reprinted in Peter Singer, *Applied Ethics* (Oxford University Press, 1986).

5. Rosalind Hursthouse, *Beginning Lives* (Oxford: Blackwell, 1987), p. 88.

6. Ian C. M. Fairweather, 'Abortion: Christian traditions not unanimous', *Abortion in Debate* (Edinburgh: Church of Scotland, St Andrew Press), p. 77.

7. Fairweather, 'Abortion', p. 78. The Pope's encyclical letter of 25 March 1995, *Evangelium Vitae* (Dublin: Veritas), p. 103ff. It was reported in October 1999 that the Catholic Church in Scotland had paid a 12-year-old girl to keep her baby rather than have an abortion even though social workers and teachers had urged it. The Church has a scheme to support pregnant women as an alternative to abortion and claims to have saved 200 babies since it was launched in 1997.

8. Ronald Dworkin, *Life's Dominion* (London: HarperCollins, 1993), p. 35ff. The statements on p. 82 about the effects of abortion are taken from Hursthouse, *Lives*, p. 19. But other women apparently find the decision to abort quite easy: Pipes, *Understanding*, p. 6.

9. Quoted by Joseph Fletcher, *Situation Ethics* (London: SCM Press, 1960), p. 155.

10. Daniel Callahan, 'The new ruling' in Feinberg (ed.), *Problem*, p. 195. Ronald Dworkin discusses the Roe v. Wade case in detail and how the decision relates to the Constitution of the USA. In general, one of the problems is that there are at least two views of the Constitution, one holding that it enshrines moral principles that judges interpret, and the other that it is relative to its time and circumstances and not binding now. Dworkin favours the former view, but how to apply these principles to particular issues is the problem (*Life's Dominion*, p. 122ff.).

11. *Euthanasia and Clinical Practice* (The Linacre Centre, 1982), p. 396 for

statements by Pope Pius XII. Norman Autton, 'The pastor and medico-moral problems', *Expository Times*, vol. 100, no. 12 (September 1989), p. 450.

12. Anthony Kenny, *Reason and Religion* (Oxford: Blackwell, 1987), p. 166.
13. Michael Lockwood, *Moral Dilemmas in Modern Medicine* (Oxford University Press, 1985), ch. 1. In addition, the Reports of the various churches and the following books have been consulted: Richard A. Wasserstrom, *Today's Moral Problems* (New York: Macmillan, 1985); William Barclay, *Ethics in a Permissive Society* (London: Collins, 1971); J. Fletcher, *Moral Responsibility* (London: SCM Press, 1967); Jonathan Glover, *Causing Death and Saving Lives* (Harmondsworth: Penguin, 1990); M. Phillips and J. Dawson, *Doctors' Dilemmas* (Brighton: Harvester Press, 1985); R. S. Downie and K. C. Calman, *Healthy Respect* (Oxford: Oxford University Press, 1990).
14. We have seen that there is much dispute about whether or not the foetus is a person from conception and if it has rights and interests. Dworkin, however, advances the argument that we ought to rely on the sanctity of life principle, or seeing life as intrinsically valuable. While it can be argued that the sacred emanates from religon, it also has a secular basis seen in opinions about nature and art reflecting the belief that these have a sacred quality. The Humanist would accept this, and both Humanist and Christian would feel a sense of loss when euthanasia was performed or a foetus aborted. But, as we noted, the disagreement continues since both conservative and liberal interpret the intrinsic value of life differently. Hence, while we can see some unity here it seems that Dworkin has been somewhat optimistic (*Life's Dominion, passim*).

Chapter Four

1. C. Donnellan (ed.), *Crime and Justice*, vol. 7 (Cambridge: Independence, 1995). For the reference to Hobbes, I am indebted to Gary L. McDowell writing in the *Independent*, April 1995. With reference to Kant, see Tom Sorrell, *Moral Theory and Capital Punishment* (Oxford: Blackwell, 1987).
2. *When the State Kills* (London: Amnesty International Publications, 1989), p. 13.
3. *Hansard Parliamentary Debates*, vol. 23, issue 1243 (London: HMSO, 11 May 1982). See Sorrell, *Moral Theory*, ch. 2, for a full discussion.
4. F. E. Zimring and G. Hawkins, *Capital Punishment and the American Agenda* (Cambridge University Press, 1986), p. 15.
5. Raoul Berger, *Death Penalties* (Cambridge MA: Harvard University Press, 1999), p. 176f.
6. *When the State Kills*, p. 229.
7. *Hansard* (1987).
8. Zimring and Hawkins, *Capital Punishment*, p. 180.

9. *Exploring the Faith*, unit 15, p. 19 (November 1988). This course in endorsed by the Baptist, Methodist and United Reformed Churches.

10. Sorell, *Moral Theory*, p. 52f. A. J. P. Kenny, in 'The balance of justice' (*Blackfriars*, October 1960, pp. 356–63), challenges the metaphors of balance and payment upon which retribution is based.

11. Sorell, *Moral Theory*, p. 94. With respect to cruel and unusual punishment, those who framed the USA Constitution did not even consider that flogging was cruel as it and other punishments were commonplace in the eighteenth century. The Eighth Amendment does not say what cruel and unusual punishment is, nor does it oppose hanging or electrocution, or state that the death penalty is cruel. Sorell, *Moral Theory*, p. 127; Ronald Dworkin, *Life's Dominion* (London: HarperCollins, 1993), p. 127.

12. Sorell, *Moral Theory*, p. 161.

Chapter Five

1. John Ferguson, *War and Peace in the World's Religions* (London: Sheldon Press, 1977), p. 56.

2. Ferguson, *War and Peace*, p. 94.

3. Ferguson, *War and Peace*, p. 103. Does Psalm 149 justify war? It was used to support the Thirty Years' War and by Thomas Muntzer to incite the peasant to rebellion in the Peasants' war. Spiritual warfare is indicated in 2 Corinthians 10:3–4, which contrasts with Psalm 149 which refers to two-edged swords in their hands.

4. Ferguson, *War and Peace*, p. 104.

5. Richard Jones, *Groundwork of Christian Ethics* (London: Epworth Press, 1984), p. 89; Augustine, *City of God* (Harmondsworth: Penguin, 1972), p. 32; Thomas Aquinas, *Summa Theologiae*, tr. English Dominicans (Eyre and Spottiswoode, 1963–75), see *Secunda Secundae* on the just war (questions 10–11 and 40).

6. Clive Barrett, *Peace Together* (Cambridge: James Clarke & Co., 1987), p. 59. Gandhi used the word *satyagraha*, that is, 'the force of truth', to describe non-violent resistance. Peter Bishop, having examined in detail the work of both Gandhi and Martin Luther King, proposes that we should allow an enemy to overrun the country and oppose by non-violent resistance. It is a controversial proposal and relies on the difficulty for the conquerors to rule a country without the consent of the subjects. We have said that it is unlikely that non-violence would succeed with governments which are not amenable to moral pressure, as occurred with Gandhi and King. Peter Bishop, *A Technique of Loving* (London: SCM Press, 1981).

7. Stanley Windass, *Christianity versus Violence* (London: Sheed & Ward, 1964), p. 43.

8. Francis Clark, 'Religion and the two World Wars', unit 30 of *War and Society* (Milton Keynes: Open University Press, 1973), p. 66.

9. Barrett, *Peace*, p. 86ff.
10. Gary Werskey, unit 31 of *War in Our Own Day* (Milton Keynes: Open University Press, 1973), p. 36.
11. See the present writer's *Journey into Apartheid* (London: Epworth Press, 1989). See also Desmond Tutu's views in *The World Religions Reader*, ed. G. Beckerlegge (London: Routledge, 1998), p. 116.
12. Werskey, *War*, p. 50.
13. Werskey, *War*, p. 53.
14. Werskey, *War*, p. 58.
15. A. Kee, *Domination or Liberation* (London: SCM Press, 1986), p. 80ff.
16. Quoted by J. H. Cone, *God of the Oppressed* (Maryknoll, NY: Orbis Books, 1997).
17. A. Fierro, *The Militant Gospel* (London: SCM Press, 1977), p. 134.
18. Roger Williamson, *Some Corner of a Foreign Field* (London: Macmillan, 1998), p. 134ff.
19. J. Ferguson, 'The peace movement', *War and Society*, unit 29, p. 57.
20. He advocates a Conference on Security and Co-operation in the Mediterranean adopting the rationale that the Europeans have been following for two decades through the Conference for Security and Co-operation, *Guardian*, 13 March 1991, p. 21.

Chapter Six

1. Jean Holm and John Bowker (eds), *Making Moral Decisions* (London: Pinter, 1998), p. 130.
2. G. Beckerlegge (ed.), *The World Religions Reader* (London: Routledge, 1998), p. 57f for the current role of Halakhah.
3. D. Gross, *1,000 Questions and Answers about Judaism* (London: Robson Books, 1987), pp. 25, 45, 237.
4. Holm and Bowker, *Decisions*, p. 102ff for analogy and example of Muhammed. Beckerlegge, *Reader*, refers to *Hadith* (story) and *sunnah* (customs) of Muhammed.
5. Holm and Bowker, *Decisions*, p. 107.
6. Holm and Bowker, *Decisions*, p. 98ff.
7. Quoted by A. Taheri, *Holy Terror* (London: Sphere Books, 1987), p. 226. On Islam and politics, see Beckerlegge, *Reader*, p. 191.
8. Holm and Bowker, *Decisions*, p. 104f. In Islam, suicide and euthanasia are forbidden (Qur'an 4:29).
9. Holm and Bowker, *Decisions*, p. 120. The sleeping foetus (*ar-raqid*) is a legal fiction (*hilah*), meaning that a pregnancy might be potentially dormant for years. It operates to shield a woman guilty of sexual sin. Today Muslims are generally opposed to such an excuse. Jean Holm and John Bowker (eds), *Women in Religion* (London: Pinter, 1994), p. 95,
10. Holm and Bowker, *Decisions*, p. 77.
11. Holm and Bowker, *Decisions*, p. 85.
12. Beckerlegge, *Reader*, p. 308ff. But abortion was legalised in India in

1971, and the killing of newborn girls has taken place. P. Morgan and C. Lawton (eds), *Ethical Issues in Six Religious Traditions* (Edinburgh University Press, 1996).

13. Beckerlegge, *Reader*, p. 308ff. for growth of political Hinduism. Some see *sati*, a wife burning herself at the death of her husband, as acceptable suicide, and euthanasia can be seen as quiet waiting for death.

14. Beckerlegge, *Reader*, p. 329ff., 344ff. for structure of the Buddha's career and teaching.

15. Beckerlegge, *Reader*, p. 350ff.

16. R. C. Zaehner (ed.), *The Concise Encyclopedia of Living Faiths* (London: Hutchinson & Co., 1979), p. 276n.

17. Holm and Bowker, *Decisions*, p. 37f.

18. Sogyal Rinpoche, *The Tibetan Book of Living and Dying* (London: Random House, 1998), p. 372ff. In the Indian tradition death can never be thought of as an escape, for karmic forces continue into the next life.

19. Conversations on tape 2 of Open University course A213.

20. Conversations on tape 2 of Open University course A213. Such violence raises the question of capital punishment and some Buddhists argue that it is appropriate.

21. Beckerlegge, *Reader*, p. 447.

22. H. McLeod, *Sikhism* (London: Penguin, 1997), p. 239.

23. O. Cole and P. S. Sambhi, *The Sikhs: Their Religious Beliefs and Practices* (Brighton: Sussex Academic Press, 2nd edn, 1995), p. 146.

24. McLeod, *Sikhism*, p. 238; Cole and Sambhi, *Sikhs*, p. 152. The BMA are in favour of prenatal screening to identify a child with a disability using ultrasound. Also diagnostic genetic tests during pregnancy can be used for foetal abnormality. *Human Genetics: Choice and Responsibility* (Oxford University Press, 1998), p. 40ff. But it should be noted that the Sikhs have a respect for life and this principle makes them wary of abortion and euthanasia. Nevertheless, the death penalty could be imposed for grave offences. Morgan and Lawton (eds), *Ethical Issues*, p. 118.

Chapter Seven

1. Rosalind Hursthouse, *Beginning Lives* (Oxford: Blackwell, 1987), p. 338.

2. J. S. Mill, *Autobiography* (Oxford University Press, 1969), ch. 5.

3. S. Anders and D. R. Cheney (eds), *The Meaning of Life* (New Jersey: Prentice-Hall, 1980), p. 12. Compare Bryan Magee, *The Great Philosophers* (Oxford University Press, 1988), p. 71.

4. Robert Campbell and Diane Collinson, *Ending Lives* (Oxford: Blackwell, 1988), p. 59. A. Schopenhauer, *The World as Will and Representation* (2 vols), tr. E. F. J. Payne (Dover, 1966), vol. 1, p. 399ff.

5. Quoted by J. O. Hanfling, *The Quest for Meaning* (Oxford: Blackwell,

1987), p. 31. T. Nagel, 'The Absurd', *Journal of Philosophy*, LXVIII, 20, 1971.

6. Phillipa Foot, 'Euthanasia' in *Philosophy and Public Affairs* (Oxford: Blackwell, 1977), vol. 6, no. 2.

7. Campbell and Collinson, *Ending Lives*, p. 73.

8. See Hanfling, *Quest*, ch. 5 for the working out of this in detail.

9. Hanfling, *Quest*, chs 6–10. Readings from the various philosophers are found in J. O. Hanfling (ed.), *Life and Meaning* (Oxford: Blackwell, 1987), and in Anders and Cheney, *Meaning*.

10. Hursthouse, *Lives*, p. 331.

11. Hanfling, *Life*, chs 6 and 7 for Rousseau's writing; also Rousseau's *Discourse on Inequality*, ed. M. Cranston (Oxford University Press, 1984).

12. Mill, *Autobiography*.

13. Hanfling, *Life*, ch. 10 for F. H. Bradley's writing; also F. H. Bradley, *Ethical Studies* (Oxford: Clarendon Press, 1927).

14. Hanfling, *Quest*, ch. 3.

15. For more detailed discussion of these objections see Hanfling, *Quest*, chs 3 and 4. For further study see supplementary reading list.

Chapter Eight

1. *Hamlet*, Act 5, Scene 11; Tennyson's *In Memoriam*. That belief in God gives meaning to life is accepted – by 44 per cent in Britain and 70 per cent in N. Ireland, according to a 1987 survey. *Codewatching: Viewers, Religion and Television* (London: John Libbey & Co. Ltd, 1988), p. 46.

2. Charles Darwin, *Autobiography* (London: Collins, 1958), pp. 139, 141. In the second edition of *The Origin of Species* (1859), Darwin wrote: 'There is a grandeur in this view of life, with its several powers, having been originally breathed by a Creator into a few forms or into one' (p. 121). See also A. Desmond and J. Moore, *Darwin* (Harmondsworth: Penguin, 1992).

3. Darwin, *Autobiography*, pp. 14, 27, 138, 152.

4. John Greer, *Evolution and God* (London: Christian Education Movement, 1979), p. 23.

5. Ian G. Barbour, *Issues in Science and Religion* (London: SCM Press, 1966), p. 90. Jacques Monod argues that our knowledge of genetics confirms 'chance' development. But Mary Hesse says that his argument has extra-scientific assumptions at every crucial point. See C. A. Russell, *Cross-Currents* (London: IVP, 1985).

6. John Davy, 'The evolution of Evolution', *Observer* magazine, 8 February 1970, p. 10ff. Richard Dawkins, one of the prominent neo-Darwinists and arch critic of religion, would not agree. I have tried to deal with some of his arguments in *The God, Man, World Triangle: A Dialogue Between Science and Religion* (London: Macmillan, 1998). Lack of space prevents discussion here.

7. Sir Karl Popper, World Philosophy Congress in Brighton, 1988; *Guardian*, 29 August 1988. Compare Bronowski, *The Common Sense of Science* (Heinemann, 1982), p. 72f. The whole question of the causal link between events was dealt with by Hume, who concluded that all we can say is that we observe that one thing follows another, e.g. night follows day etc. The idea of 'chance' rather than 'purpose' does not necessarily rule out order. Chance mutations over a long period of time can produce a highly organised form of life. See Keith Ward, *The Turn of the Tide* (London: BBC publications, 1986), p. 34.

8. Paul Davis, *God and the New Physics* (London: J. M. Dent & Sons, 1983), p. 168. Stephen Hawking refers to the possibility of life on this planet depending upon the delicate balance of the basic forces of nature and on specific initial conditions. He defines the anthropic principle: 'Things are as they are because we are.' See the full discussion of this principle in my book *The God, Man, World Triangle*, p. 78ff.

9. Davis, *God*, p. 55.

10. Wittgenstein said: 'The whole modern conception of the world is founded on the illusion that the so-called laws of nature are the explanations of natural phenomena', and added that 'even if all possible scientific questions had been answered the problems of life would remain completely untouched'. Bryan Magee, *The Great Philosophers* (Oxford University Press, 1988), p. 129. Schopenhauer would have agreed with Wittgenstein.

11. J. O. Hanfling, 'Body and mind', *Philosophical Problems* (Milton Keynes: Open University, 1980), units 1–2, p. 45f.

12. *Immortality or Extinction?* (London: Macmillan, 1982).

13. *The National Review*, 14 October 1988, p. 38ff.

14. *Beginning Lives* (Oxford: Blackwell, 1987), p. 38ff.

Suggestions for Further Reading

Aristotle, *Nicomachean Ethics* (Harmondsworth: Penguin, 1976).

Aristotle, *Eudemian Ethics* (Oxford University Press, 1982).

Karen Armstrong, *Holy War: The Crusades and Their Impact on Today's World* (London: Macmillan, 1988).

Thomas Aquinas, *Summa Theologiae*, tr. English Dominicans (Eyre and Spottiswoode, 1963–1975), *Secunda Secundae*.

Augustine, *City of God*, tr. H. Bettenson (Harmondsworth: Penguin, 1972).

Ian Barbour, *Issues in Science and Religion* (London: HarperCollins Inc., 1971).

T. L. Beauchamp and J. F. Childress, *Principles of Biomedical Ethics* (Oxford University Press, 1970).

G. Beckerlegge (ed.), *The World Religions Reader* (London: Routledge, 1998). Contains texts of the religions.

Peter Bishop, *A Technique of Loving* (London: SCM Press, 1981).

J. Bentham, *An Introduction to the Principles of Morals and Legislation*, ed. J. Burns and H. Hart (Oxford: Clarendon Press, 1996).

F. H. Bradley, 'A social morality' in J. O. Hanfling (ed.), *Life and Meaning* (Oxford: Blackwell, 1987), pp. 189–218.

Robert Campbell and Diane Collinson, *Ending Lives* (Oxford: Blackwell, 1988).

Albert Camus, *The Myth of Sisyphus* (Harmondsworth: Penguin, 1990).

W. O. Cole and P. S. Sambhi, *The Sikhs: Their Religious Beliefs and Practices* (London: Routledge and Kegan Paul, 1978).

E. Conze, *Buddhist Scriptures* (Harmondsworth: Penguin, 1959).

H. G. Coward, J. J. Lipner and K. K. Young, *Hindu Ethics: Purity, Abortion and Euthanasia* (New York: SUNY Press, 1989).

R. Crawford, *Journey into Apartheid* (London: Epworth Press, 1989).

R. Crawford, *The God, Man, World Triangle* (London: Macmillan, 1998).

Charles Darwin, *Autobiography* (London: Collins, 1958; originally published 1887).

Charles Darwin, *The Origin of Species* (1859; Cambridge MA: Harvard University Press, 1964).

P. Davies, *The Cosmic Blueprint: New Discoveries in the Creative Ability to Order the Universe* (London: Heinemann, 1987).

John Donne, *Biathanatos*, ed. E. W. Sullivan II (University of Delaware Press, 1984).

Richard Dawkins, *The Blind Watchmaker* (London: Penguin, 1990).

Richard Dawkins, *The Selfish Gene* (Oxford University Press, 1989).

A. Desmond and J. Moore, *Darwin* (Harmondsworth: Penguin, 1992).

W. D. Doniger, *The Laws of Manu* (Harmondsworth: Penguin, 1991).

Niles Eldredge, *Reinventing Darwin: The Great Evolutionary Debate* (London: Weidenfeld & Nicolson, 1995).

John Ferguson, *War and Peace in the World's Religions* (London: Sheldon Press, 1977).

P. Foot, *Virtues and Vices* (Oxford: Blackwell, 1979).

Robin Gill (ed.), *Euthanasia and the Churches* (London: Cassell, 1998).

Robin Gill, *A Textbook of Christian Ethics* (Edinburgh: T. & T. Clark, 1995).

J. Glover, *Causing Death and Saving Lives* (Harmondsworth: Penguin, 1990).

J. O. Hanfling, *The Quest for Meaning* (Oxford: Blackwell, 1987).

J. O. Hanfling (ed.), *Life and Meaning* (Oxford: Blackwell, 1987).

S. Hawking, *A Brief History of Time* (London: Bantam, 1995).

D. Hume, 'Of suicide' in *Applied Ethics*, ed. P. Singer (Oxford University Press, 1986), p. 19ff.

D. Hume, *Dialogues Concerning Natural Religion* (Harmondsworth: Penguin, 1990 edn).

Rosalind Hursthouse, *Beginning Lives* (Oxford: Blackwell, 1987).

I. Kant, *Lectures on Ethics* (London: Methuen, 1930).

I. Kant, *Religion within the Limits of Reason Alone* (New York: Harper & Row, 1960).

Koran, tr. N. J. Dawood (Harmondsworth: Penguin, 1990).

W. H. McLeod (ed. and tr.), *Textual Sources for the Study of Sikhism* (Manchester University Press, 1984).

W. H. McLeod, *Sikhism* (London: Penguin, 1997).

J. S. Mill, *Utilitarianism* (London: Fontana, 1962).

J. S. Mill, *Autobiography* (Oxford University Press, 1969).

J. R. Moore, *The Post-Darwinian Controversies* (Oxford University Press, 1979).

Thomas Nagel, 'The absurd' in Hanfling (ed.), *Life and Meaning*, pp. 49–59.

J. Polkinghorne, *Scientists as Theologians* (London: SPCK, 1996).

Karl Popper, *Conjecture and Refutations* (London: Routledge & Kegan Paul, 1963).

J. Rachels, *The End of Life* (Oxford University Press, 1986).

J. Rawls, *A Theory of Justice* (Oxford University Press, 1999).

J.-P. Sartre, *The Reprieve* (Harmondsworth: Penguin, 1990) and in *Reader*, pp. 219–26.

M. Schlick, 'The meaning of life' in Hanfling (ed.), *Life and Meaning*, pp. 60–73.

Arthur Schopenhauer, *The World as Will and Representation* (2 vols), tr. E. F. J. Payne (Dover, 1966).

P. Singer, *Applied Ethics* (Oxford University Press, 1986).

Tom Sorell, *Moral Theory and Capital Punishment* (Oxford: Blackwell, 1987).

R. Stannard, *Science and the Renewal of Belief* (London: SCM Press, 1982).

W. S. Towner, *How God Deals with Evil* (Pennsylvania: Westminster Press, 1976).

Upanishads, tr. Juan Mascaro (Harmondsworth: Penguin, 1965).

Keith Ward, *Chance and Necessity* (Oxford: OneWorld, 1996).

B. Williams, *Ethics and the Limits of Philosophy* (London: Fontana, 1985).

B. Williams, *An Introduction to Ethics* (Oxford University Press, 1972).

R. C. Zaehner, *Encyclopedia of Living Faiths* (London: Hutchinson, 1979).

Index

221